A 12-STEP PROGRAMME TO REMAKE BRITAIN

The Alternative Manifesto

A 12-STEP PROGRAMME TO REMAKE BRITAIN

Eamonn Butler

GIBSON SQUARE

London

This edition first published in by

Gibson Square

UK Tel: +44 (0)20 7096 1100
     Fax: +44 (0)20 7993 2214

US Tel: +1 646 216 9813
     Fax: +1 646 216 9488

Eire Tel: +353 (0)1 657 1057

     info@gibsonsquare.com
     www.gibsonsquare.com

     ISBN 9781906142698

CONTENTS

ACKNOWLEDGEMENTS

I thank the following for their ideas, suggestions and criticism: Adam Smith Institute Fellow Tim Ambler; Mark Baillie of the International Policy Network; Anthony Browne, Policy Director at the Mayor of London's office; Iain Dale, publisher of *Total Politics*; Matthew Elliott of the Taxpayers Alliance; Andrew Haldenby of Reform; David Green of Civitas; Jill Kirby of the Centre for Policy Studies; Dan Lewis of the Economic Research Council; Andrew Lilico of Policy Exchange; Tim Montgomerie of Conservative Home; Neil O'Brien of Policy Exchange; Madsen Pirie of the Adam Smith Institute; Mathew Sinclair of the Taxpayers Alliance; Gabriel Stein of Lombard Street Research; Corin Taylor of the Institute of Directors; Robert Wheelan of the New Model School Company; Eben Wilson of Main Communications.

Thanks also to Steve Bettison and Charlotte Bowyer of the Adam Smith Institute for their research and fact checking, and to my wife Christine for her expert assistance in preparing the typescript.

1

WHAT POLITICIANS NEED TO DO FOR US

Sometimes politicians seem to act as if they own us. Recently, for example, I saw a report from a think-tank, which proposed we should all engage in 'civic service'. Sounds good, you might suppose: we need more people helping society by voluntary work — particularly since it has become a lot harder to find volunteers recently, what with all those CRB checks that people have to go through, the numerous health and safety requirements, and the general fear of litigation if some accident does happen.

But this is not what they had in mind at all. Their idea of volunteering was not putting in something extra, over and above the obligations of citizenship — something that would be admired and welcomed, but is by no means *expected* of any of us. No, their brand of 'volunteering' would be... compulsory. School children would be forced to volunteer as part of the national curriculum. University students would be forced to do a hundred hours of community service over the course of their degree. Public servants would be given an extra week's leave so they can go out and do good works for the nation (which hardly seems like a good way to cut NHS waiting lists or to fill the gaps in our children's education). I could not bear to read any further, so I do not know what they have in mind for the rest of us.

Helping others out of the goodness of your heart is of course a good thing, and should be encouraged. But this particular form of volunteering is in fact more like conscription; it is not civic service but forced labour. It does not make the people who do it morally better, any more than slavery does. Like slavery, however, it does speak volumes about the moral view of those who would be the slave drivers.

Who are the masters?

After so many years of governments that have systematically tried to force us to live according to their metropolitan, middle-class view of the world, I really should know better. Yet I still find it astonishing that people in Westminster actually think it is right to treat us like this — as if we were mere components in some vast social machine that they were directing. After all, the reality of it is that *their* authority comes from *us*, not the other way round. We elect them to work for us and safeguard our values — not to use the power that comes with office to impose their values on us and tell us what to do.

Sometimes I wake up sweating: because it worries me that this may be the best our political system can produce. Parliament was established precisely in order to limit the power of our political leaders and bring them to account. Yet with so many seats in today's Parliament now occupied by ministers, the institution is riven by a huge conflict of interest. How can it ever bring the executive to account, when so many of its members are part of that very executive — or fancy that, if they do not rock the boat too much, they might soon become part of it? How can it represent and defend the rights and opinions of the public against the power of the executive, when the executive itself can use its legislative majority in Parliament to suspend the most basic rights and override the most deeply held of the public's opinions?

This executive power has increased, is increasing, and ought to be diminished. In part it is fed by the 24-hour news media, which naturally wants to report ministers taking instant action when issues arise — not a lengthy debate in Parliament about what is actually the best thing to do about it. In part it is the inside access that ministers have to official figures and announcements, and the temptation for them to trade that with friendly media in return for favourable coverage. In part it is the politicisation of the civil service, and the deliberate confusion between what is government and what is party. Electioneering and populism has much to do with it: promising bread and circuses today, and letting some other politicians work out how to pay for them tomorrow.

Floating voters

Perhaps the electoral system contributes to the malaise. The fact is that most of us electors do not count for very much. We live in parliamentary seats that rarely change from one party to another between ballots. Elections are won or lost in the marginal constituencies, perhaps just thirty or forty of them, out of more than six hundred. And within those marginal constituencies, it is marginal voters who will make the difference: not the majority who have solid party allegiances and are unlikely to change their vote, but the minority who have no set loyalties and may not even decide how to cast their vote until they have the ballot paper in their hand.

No, elections are decided by perhaps one or two percent of the electorate; and that is where the political parties focus their attention. They research and canvass the views of these floating voters with huge energy and precision. They pour money into the marginal constituencies. They use polls and focus groups to find out exactly what issues are of concern to the waverers, and what they think about them. Then they print election material that is designed to reinforce those same views. Floating voters will get this material, while their next-door neighbours who have fixed voting habits will get nothing. That is how precise it has become.

There is no room for ideas or principles when you are trying to convince the undecided voters that you agree with absolutely everything they think — or at least go along with as conventional wisdom. That may be why the party spin-doctors have completely lost any sense or understanding of the importance of constitutional limits on the processes of government. They believe that you say anything to get elected, and once elected, nobody can stop you doing what you 'know' is right — not the civil service, nor the courts, nor Parliament, nor any of the other institutions of state that check and balance each other.

Maybe this is all we can expect of a democracy like ours. But if it is, that frail semblance of democracy cannot last for long. Once power is concentrated at the centre, and the powerful no longer see themselves as merely the temporary and constrained custodians of authority, but its legitimate masters, then it cannot be long before democratic government morphs into executive tyranny. Sometimes it seems as if the process has already started.

The power of motivated individuals
Most MPs and candidates of my acquaintance have entered politics because they really do — or did — believe that they

could make their country a little better for everyone. If, when they get to Parliament, they act badly, it is usually because they have fallen in with a bad crowd — namely, other MPs. If they become venal, it is because there is no room for self-doubt in the rough world of politics, and they really do come to think that they are worth whatever they can screw out of the system. And of course the many perks of office are indeed hard to resist.

In a Parliament with so many fresh faces as that elected in 2010, there is a real chance to capture the enthusiasm of new MPs before the perks and protocols of office absorb them. This Parliament could — I put it no stronger than that — be a hugely reforming Parliament. Its new members may recognise, better than those who have been institutionalised there for years, the importance of asserting the rights and freedoms of the people who elected them. They may just be brave enough to take proper control over the executive, even defying the orders of their own whips and party officials.

One cannot expect politicians in a ruling party to rush to impose restraints on their own power. Yet there may be just enough of them in senior positions to do just this, motivated only by the recognition that it is, ultimately, the right thing to do. After all, a decade and more of centralised power, of the politicisation of the institutions of the state, of spin and media manipulation brought the political class as low as it has ever been, at least since the Civil War or maybe the Peasants' Revolt. They can surely see that something different is needed if we are to trust them — and more than that, respect them — ever again.

It will take a measure of bravery that is not common in politicians to give up power and devolve it to the localities and indeed to ordinary citizens. It will take steel for ministers to tell the media that they do not have an instant solution to every problem that arises, and that they are going to think about it so that they come up with the right solution. Or even more unusually, that they are going to let Parliament and the nation take time to debate it, and leave the decision to them. Or more sensationally still, that they think the issue is no business of politicians at all and should be left to individuals themselves to sort out. It will take strong personalities to defend and uphold the civil rights of the public and the long-sighted principles of justice when the red-tops are leading the baying mob. But these are things — limits on authority, parliamentary debate, the liberty to run our own lives, and the rule of law — which earlier generations have fought and died to defend, such is their importance to our democracy. Perhaps there are enough politicians who will recognise that importance, and do something to assert it, even if it means giving up their own power.

With no unified constitution, an executive branch that dominates Parliament, a presidential style of government (except that our presidential-style prime ministers are not directly elected by the public) and a legislature that can re-write any law from the Magna Carta to the Bill of Rights and beyond, this hope may be forlorn. If it is to happen, incoming ministers will have to move quickly to break up and devolve their central power, and put it, as the IRA said of its weapons caches, 'beyond use'.

Perhaps the French statesman and writer Frédéric Bastiat best summed up the task facing reformers. 'And now that the legislators and do-gooders have futilely inflicted so many systems upon society,' he wrote, 'may they finally end where they should have begun. May they reject all systems. And try liberty.'

2

THE ECONOMY

We're all f***ed. I'm f***ed, you're f***ed. It's the biggest cock-up ever. We're all completely f***ed. So said top Whitehall fixer Sir Richard Mottram in 2002 as the 9/11 'good day to bury bad news' spin scandal finally exploded. Sir Richard has long since retired to the great civil-service pension in the sky — a modest £2.7 million package, giving him a tax-free lump sum of £335,000 plus £110,000 a year (which he ekes out with a handful of quango and company board directorships). But his words would apply equally well to the UK economy today. Our recession has been deeper and longer than anyone's, and we have only survived it by piling up debts even bigger than America's. There is no escaping the fact that we are, indeed, all f***ed.

Made by Gordon Brown

The financial crisis is not the only father of our misfortunes. The main reason for our embarrassed state is that our finances had been systematically raped by Gordon Brown's wild overspending long before the crash hit us. As the radical Conservative MP Douglas Carswell said on his blog, no matter what government is in power, public spending just grows. In 1950 it stood at just £100 billion. By 1980 it had tripled. Even Mrs Thatcher left it slightly higher than she found it. Then from 1990 it soared, nearly tripling again to over £676 billion today. And the steepest rise since the Second World War came in just a decade — when Gordon Brown broke free of his 1997 election promise to match Conservative spending plans and started to do his own thing. Thanks to 80-odd stealth taxes, Brown was able to increase the amount of tax we pay by half as much again. Yet even that was not enough to balance the books, since spending rose even faster; and the government had to borrow more and more to fill the budget hole.

Then, when the financial crisis did hit and we needed cash to bail out the banks, the cupboard was bare. Over-borrowed Britain had to borrow still more, leaving us with no shelter against the global storm.

Even by the government's own forecasts, the total amount it owes — to investors from abroad and those of us at home who have been gullible enough to hand it our savings for premium bonds and the like — will soon reach double its pre-crisis levels. In 2009/10 it totalled £798 billion, an amount equal to 55% of the whole country's yearly income (Gross Domestic Product, or GDP). The interest on that alone will soon reach £44 billion, more than the defence budget. By 2014/15, the national debt will hit £1,473 billion says the Treasury, equal to 78% of GDP. But government forecasts are always rose-tinted: most economists figure that by 2015 the national debt will be closer to 100% of GDP, and still rising.

The optimists dismiss this as no problem: after all, many families borrow three or four times their income in order to buy a house. And in 1950 the national debt was 250%, as it was after Waterloo. So very high borrowing is neither irrational nor unprecedented. But after Waterloo we were at least borrowing to pay off a twelve-year war against Napoleon, and in 1950 we had to stump up the cost of a five-year struggle to save the world from fascism (it took us sixty years, until 2006, before we handed over the last instalment). Likewise, when families take out a mortgage, they do end up with a house to show for it. Unfortunately there is no victory over tyranny, no house to show for today's borrowing binge. All it has bought us is even more extravagant government spending and a collection of decrepit nationalised banks.

Yet the borrowing just goes on. To put it in context, the national debt pretty well started with the Napoleonic wars, about 200 years ago. From then until the year 200, the total debt run up by all the governments in that period amounted to £300 billion. Right now, the government plans to borrow that amount, not over the next 200 years, but over the next 20 months!

What economists call the 'deficit' is the difference between what the government pulls in each year (from taxes, licence fees and the like), and what it spends (on the civil service, public services and so on). If you or I were deep in debt, we would try not to keep adding to it by borrowing still more each year. Politicians, though, seem quite unbothered by annual deficits that are growing the national debt at the rate of an extra £20 million an hour.

In the financial year 2009/10, the Treasury expected to borrow another £178 billion, an amount equal to £3,000 for every man, woman and child in the UK. (Though when the books are finally closed, the deficit will probably turn out to be more like £200 billion.) In 2010/11 they plan to borrow as much again. The following year they plan to borrow another £2,300 for each of us, then a further £1,920 the year after that. This is the highest annual borrowing in the developed world, the highest our peacetime history, and roughly twice the deficit in 1976, when the UK had to go to the IMF for an emergency bailout.

With debts piling up year after year, it is no wonder that Standard & Poor's, one of the big credit ratings agencies, has downgraded the UK's prospects to 'negative', because our finances were deteriorating faster than expected. The Conservatives' 2009 conference promise to cut spending was probably the only thing that spared us an even worse downgrade. Two rival agencies, Fitch and Moody's, have even hinted that the UK could lose its cherished AAA rating — a sure 'sell' signal to overseas investors — because its budget position is the worst of any advanced country.

That seems a shrewd call. The UK's debts are increasing faster than its income — which actually shrank by 6% over the 2007-09 crisis period — making them harder and harder to pay off. Already, every infant born in the UK inherits a debt of £13,000. Even under the government's forecasts, that debt will keep rising as far as the eye can see.

Meanwhile, businesses have lost money and shed staff, so the government has less tax revenue coming in to balance the books. Taxes from business fell about 25% in 2009, to the lowest levels in five years. In addition, more people are out of work and claiming social benefits, another headache for government bean-counters.

How bad is the UK's financial hangover?
'Official forecasts for debt are still based on optimistic assumptions that the economy will trampoline back to extremely strong growth,' says Matthew Sinclair, research director and number cruncher at the increasingly influential

TaxPayers Alliance (TPA). Indeed, the Treasury believes that our income — which shrank for nearly two years — will soon bounce back to an astonishing 3.25% from 2011/12. But 'it would be madness to form policy solely on the basis of such a sunny vision of the future,' says Sinclair. The mistakes that caused the credit crunch and the financial crisis, he argues, were rooted in a similarly rosy view of the strength of the UK economy.

In 2009 the TPA commissioned the well-respected analysts at the Centre for Economics and Business Research (CEBR) to produce a more realistic view of how our economy is faring. Being economists they rather boringly called it *Can Tax Increases Solve The United Kingdom's Public Finance Crisis?* Nevertheless, it is rather gripping stuff, if only because its conclusions are so alarming. CEBR reasons that the economy has taken a deep knock, and will grow at less than half the rate the Treasury expects. That means that the national debt will reach not 78% of GDP in 2014/15, but something around 95%. Standard & Poor's reckon it could actually reach 100% by then, leaving the government owing more than the whole country earns in a year, or twice the government's own annual income.

The really alarming thing is that economists see no sign of the debt mountain crumbling. CEBR calculates that by 2017/18 it will still be rising, and growing as a proportion of GDP, with no end in sight.

Penalties for partial financial statements

Maybe you think things cannot get worse than this. Sadly, they actually *are* worse than this. The official figures tell only half the story about government debt. They are, in fact, a complete snow-job.

One big-ticket item you will not find on the government's books is the cost of all those new schools and hospitals built under the Private Finance Initiative (PFI). The idea of PFI was to get private consortia to design, build, own and operate big infrastructure projects, because they were better at it than civil servants. Then the government would simply purchase as many school places or hospital beds as it needed: all very efficient. But Gordon Brown simply turned PFI into a giant mortgage scheme, allowing him to boast about a massive building spree without having to find the cash upfront — and without it appearing on the accounts.

Unfortunately PFI projects do run into trouble, like the failed Metronet scheme for London's tube system, which left taxpayers with a £410 million bill. The Treasury reckons that PFI failures over the next eighteen months might cost us another £2 billion, but that may be wishful thinking. Because of this risk, Brooks Newmark, a Conservative MP with a background in finance, says PFI projects should go on the government's balance sheet of assets and liabilities as a large potential cost. In fact a £139 billion potential cost, as he estimates in his 2009 Centre for Policy Studies paper, *The Hidden Debt Bombshell*.

By comparison, Network Rail's enormous borrowing looks like a real tiddler, at £22 billion. That does not appear on the books either, because the government conveniently defines them as a private company. Maybe, but if it runs out of money, you can be sure that taxpayers will have to stump up. And in times like these, even something as big as Network Rail can easily run out of money.

Fifty times larger still is the money we have promised to pay in pensions to the likes of Sir Richard Mottram — plus teachers, NHS workers, police, fire brigades and others. In their 2009 Policy Exchange report *Public Sector Pensions*, Neil Record and James Mackenzie Smith calculate that this amounts to another £1,104 billion that should appear in the government's books — though with people living longer, it could work out at much more than that.

Then there are those bank bailouts, a staggering £142 billion worth, according to the Office for National Statistics (ONS). Now the government owns two of our major banks, RBS and Lloyds, and the taxpayer is picking up the cost of their bad loans. The cost is huge: equivalent to 3.5% of GDP according to the Treasury, though the IMF believes it is three times more, at 9.3% of GDP. Of the two, I know which one I would believe, unpleasant though the bottom line is: a liability of £130 billion, or £2,100 per man, woman and child in the UK.

When Brooks Newmark added up all these hidden time-bombs, he found that the true size of the government's debt is not £825 billion, but nearly three times more, at £2,220 billion — a debt of nearly £150,000 for a family of four. That is more than the average household mortgage; and as I say, at least with a mortgage your family get a house out of the deal.

But I reckon this still underestimates the debt, which is in fact *twice* that amount. Former England rugby player, author of *Crap: A Guide To Politics* and now veteran actuary and pension expert Terry Arthur has run some figures on the state pension that we all get when we retire. Of course, there are a lot of us, and we are living longer (men can expect to live for 77 years, women 82 years), so there is a lot of money to pay out. Some £2,220 billion, according to Terry. When you add that in, it *exactly doubles* Newmark's total, taking it to £4,440 billion. And if you added in the total liabilities of the nation-alised banks — £2,000 billion in the case of the Royal Bank of Scotland (RBS) and another £1,000 for HBOS/Lloyds — really, the numbers are very scary indeed.

With any luck the government, as the main shareholder, will not run the banks so appallingly that they become utterly worthless (though you never know). And most of those pension payments will only fall due years from now. Yet if you or I were asked how much we owed, we would include our long-term debts like mortgages, and would not just put down what we thought we might, if the sun shone and everything worked out well, stand to pay out this year. Companies too have to identify their total future liabilities. In fact, if the government were a private company, they would be put in jail for not stating their full debts: and why, indeed, should politicians and Treasury officials escape such penalties?

The unlikely medicine of international accounting standards
A government in denial about what it owes is not a good basis from which to sort the problem out. In a 1996 Adam Smith Institute report *The Kiwi Effect*, Robert O'Quinn and Nigel Ashford showed how New Zealand's (Labour) government had sorted out its dismal finances by adopting international accounting standards that gave a clear picture of its liabilities. In stark contrast, the UK's (Labour) government systematically resisted using the International Financial Reporting Standards (IRFS) that it demands of everyone else, precisely in order to keep spending without it showing.

The first step towards putting the public debt right is for the government to adopt international accounting standards and fess up its 'off balance sheet' liabilities — that is, its under-the-counter debts. The Treasury will never come clean on this, of course, and even the Office for National Statistics

(ONS) is not independent enough for the job: so an independent panel of commercial auditors should decide what liabilities should be included and how they should be valued.

Whatever is included, the size of the government's debt is important to us all. Large-scale government borrowing drives up the cost and reduces the availability of loans to businesses, making it harder for them to invest and expand and get us out of this mess. If the public finances seem so dire that people fear the government might cannot repay its debts, investors round the world will pull the plug or demand higher interest payments. That makes it even more expensive for us to borrow in the future or to pay off the debt we already have, leaving us with less cash to spend on public services. In 2010/11, for example, the cost of servicing government debt will be £44 billion, as big as the defence budget. If lenders start playing hardball, it could get even higher.

If lenders pulled their money out of the UK and selling sterling, the value of the pound (already at record lows) would fall still further, making imports more expensive. Indeed, the government is already running out of people to lend it money. Recent auctions have failed to find buyers for Treasury bonds. The only thing propping up the debt-creation machine has been the Bank of England printing money and using it to buy government IOUs.

Maybe we should not get too worked up about all this. We are not in as deep a pickle as Japan got into in the 1990s. Other countries have debt levels that seem as big as ours. As Adam Smith said, there is a great deal of ruin in a nation. And in the 1980s and again in the 1990s, the UK government's budget went from deficit to surplus in five years or so, thanks to surging growth.

Yet it is the sheer-cliff growth of today's debt that is the worry. On most people's predictions, things are just going to get worse and worse. Like any family with large debts to pay, we will have to get used to living more frugally. The painful fact is that other parts of the world, like the Middle East and Asia, will be powering ahead while we penny-pinch to pay our bills. The world financial balance has changed.

Again like any family, the only sensible courses of action are obvious. We have to earn more, or spend less, or some combination of the two. (Though governments have a third option, of simply printing money in order to pay their bills. When overseas investors cotton on to this, though, they might reckon that your promises and your cash are now both worthless, and leave you well and truly bust.)

In terms of earning more, the government hopes that a big upturn in business will restore the country's fortunes, and its own along with them. Yet even on staggeringly optimistic Treasury forecasts, that will not happen soon. Economic growth is a key part of getting us back into the black; but it is not enough to balance the books on its own.

A hair of the taxation dog?
Another option is that the government can try to cover its costs by making taxpayers dig deeper. You can see why politicians are drawn to this idea: it effortlessly soothes their budgeting headaches. Yet it is an utterly stupid idea, because it brings on budget migraines for the rest of us — and it is the rest of us, the private sector, who generate the nation's wealth. Report after report from academic economists, from the European Central Bank, and from the Organisation for Economic Co-operation and Development (the rich countries' economics think-tank) have shown that high taxes

choke off economic growth. A spluttering economy would hardly generate the cash we need to pay off the government's debts and re-invest in our productive businesses.

Probably the *most* stupid idea is the 50p income tax rate on higher earners. The Treasury say it will pull in £2.4 billion a year, which is a lot (though it hardly dents a deficit of £178 billion). But the respected Institute for Fiscal Studies (IFS) thinks that highly optimistic; and my guess is that the higher rate will produce *falling* receipts for the Treasury as higher earners simply work less, hire more devious accountants, and move their money or themselves abroad. Indeed, the CEBR/TPA report reckons that the 50p tax will reduce economic growth by 0.4% and increase public borrowing by £1.8 billion over the next ten years.

The top ten percent of UK earners pay about a quarter of the total tax revenue, but they are also highly mobile. Upping sticks makes perfect sense when the 50p tax rate, combined with other stealth changes to national insurance and tax allowances, mean that people earning just over £100,000 see nearly two-thirds of their earnings (61.5%) disappear in tax. Already the relocation companies are rubbing their hands with glee. Savills, the upmarket estate agent, held two over-subscribed seminars in 2009 after the 50p rate was announced, advising City folk how to move to Switzerland. Geneva offices are about a third of the price of London too, all of which might explain why Blue Crest Capital Management, one of the top five financial funds in Europe, plans to move its entire business there, along with fifty of its top earners too. Finance is a mobile business: it may be nice to be in the bustle of London, but with a good internet connection, you can manage investment funds from just about anywhere in the world — and Switzerland's tax rates are half ours.

All of which makes Britain's arbitrary taxes on non-doms — Americans and others who live and work in the UK but pay taxes back home — all the more astonishing. George Osborne, as Conservative finance spokesman, started this back in 2007, saying non-doms should pay an annual £25,000 contribution to public services — which gave the government an excuse to bring in its own £30,000 charge, payable regardless of the person's income. By definition, though, non-doms are mobile people. Right now we cannot afford to lose them and the business they bring in to the UK, and a £30,000 poll tax on them hardly amounts to a welcome mat. Remember the days, a decade ago, when the World Economic Forum (the ones who hold the annual conference for world leaders in Davos, Switzerland) rated the UK as the world's fourth most competitive economy? Well, now we are down to thirteenth, thanks to our huge debts and high taxes. We have to attract more good people, not spit in their faces. The non-dom tax should go.

As should the 50p rate. Osborne says it will have to stay for at least two years. No doubt the Conservatives do not want to be thought of as helping the rich in these hard times; perhaps the damage caused by the 50p rate has to become obvious before they dare abolish it. They would be better to spare us the damage entirely.

The Treasury, of course, will not help them. Its calculations work on a static model of taxation that suggests if you put the rate up by a quarter, you get a quarter as much money again rolling in to the Exchequer. But high taxes change people's behaviour. In the 1970s, that with tax rates as high as 83% (or 98% if you were misguided enough to earn your money by investing in UK industry and jobs), many job creators simply downed tools or went abroad. Raising income tax to 100%, would not produce any revenue at all, because absolutely everyone would down tools or go abroad. We need a dynamic model of taxation for setting tax policy. We should appoint a panel of independent economists to work one out, and to tell policymakers where higher tax rates will kill business and lead to falling returns. That is not a job that Treasury mandarins would be likely to do very willingly.

Other crazy book-balancing ideas include raising VAT to 20%, increasing the basic rate of income tax, and upping company taxes. All would bring in money — at first. But all are profoundly mistaken.

The trouble with VAT — alongside the huge administrative burden it places on small companies– is that it is regressive. Despite exemptions for food and children's clothes, rich people can afford to pay a bit more VAT, while poorer people cannot. It already creates a back-pocket economy in which people pay cash rather than see a large amount added onto their bill, and as such, makes criminals of far too many people.

As for raising income tax and company taxes along with it, the CEPR/TPA report again shows this to be a mistake. Raising the basic tax rate to 25p and corporation tax to 41% would at first net the Treasury around £15 billion — again, not much of a dent on the deficit, though still a fair chunk of change. But it would leave consumers poorer, and hit business, including exports. At the end of the decade, we would see a 6.1% fall in GDP and a £33 billion increase in borrowing.

The economic picture is bad enough. We could do without such long-term damage, even if it brings short-term comfort to the Treasury. It is not a good idea to slap additional taxes, on either producers or consumers, when unemployment is high and rising. According to a Confederation of British Industry (CBI) survey at the end of 2009, half of the UK's companies plan to freeze pay this year — that is on top of the recruitment freeze that two-thirds of them imposed this year, and on top of the job losses that were felt almost everywhere. Not surprisingly, the CEPR/TPA report says that unemployment will probably rise above the government's 'optimistic' forecasts, to 3.2 million next year. But if you take a 'pessimistic' view, they say, it could rise as high as 3.8 million.

Quite a number of Westminster economists of my acquaintance *do* take a pessimistic view. Dr Andrew Lilico is one of the most prominent. Andrew is an economist's economist. He has a degree from Oxford and two higher degrees from London. He talks, eats, drinks, breathes and probably dreams economics, which may be why Policy Exchange made him their chief economist. So he ought to be worth listening to on this sort of thing. As I visit the think-tank's Westminster HQ to see its boss Neil O'Brien, he pulls me over to his computer screen. Unsurprisingly, it is full of tables and charts, and, by popping one graph on top of another, he shows me some of the uncanny similarities between the current economic downturn and the 1990s recession. Tracing the graphs to their peak, the number comes out at — yes, 3.8 million. Maybe it is just coincidence, but if I were a gambler, that is what I would put my money on. He thinks the Treasury is right to the extent that the economy will race ahead in 2011, so — barring accidents — the numbers will not go any higher. Still, 3.8 million is still a lot of people — and their families — to be living on the dole rather than contributing to economic recovery. It is a chilling prospect.

Civil service cuts

Our problem is not that the government is taxing too little: our problem is that the government is spending too much. Under Gordon Brown's stint as Chancellor, taxes and spending ate up more and more of the UK's income — rising faster than any other developed country. High spending is the main reason we are now broke, which is why both the IMF and the OECD have warned that we need to bring public spending under control. The IMF — and even the European Commission, for goodness' sake — agree that lower government spending and firm limits on taxing and borrowing generally produces a more lasting economic recovery than rises in tax.

Too many politicians say that we need spending cuts, but not now. We need to 'invest' our way out of this hole: we need a 'fiscal stimulus'. In other words, the government needs to spend even more. Fiscal *stimulus*? That is fiscal alcoholism: the politicians know they need to come off the borrowing booze, but say they need just one more bottle to set them up for it. Yet the economic evidence of decades shows that stimulus packages rarely raise the nation's income by more than they cost it. Grover Norquist, the fast moving, constantly networking, shoot-from-the-lip head of Americans for Tax Reform, sums it up neatly. 'Creating jobs', 'supporting industry' and all the other 'stimulus' packages are, he says, rather like quietly taking a bucket of water from one side of a lake, walking round to the other, and throwing it back in with great fanfare. At best, it does no good, and at worst, you spill a lot on the way. The money you throw into one sector has to come out of others. You might save a large manufacturing plant and its highly visible jobs, but more jobs are lost, in ones and twos, from shops, cafes, offices, and artisans who can no longer afford so many staff because their rates, taxes and national insurance have all risen.

No politician wants to talk about public spending cuts, particularly before an election. Even George Osborne's much vaunted 'blood, sweat and tears' speech at the 2009 Conservative conference outlined only £7 billion of savings — roughly enough to cover what the government was *over*-spending every fortnight. Indeed, politicians hesitate even to think about the subject, which means that they come into office completely unprepared, not knowing where it is possible to make savings without threatening essential services.

Yet radical cuts — and reforms — *are* needed. Over the five years up to 2008/09, public spending grew by about 6.7%. According to the CEBR, we must turn that figure into -1% to have any chance of levelling off the national debt by 2015/16. With inflation running at 2%, that means real budget cuts of 3% — a major reversal. But both Labour and Conservatives — recklessly — say they will ring-fence NHS spending against any cuts. But the NHS budget is huge, and if it is spared, there will have to be much bigger cuts elsewhere — maybe 10% across the board.

That would mean cutting about £50 billion of public expenditure each year, until the books balanced again. For once the TaxPayers Alliance and the Institute of Directors begin to look rather moderate. Their plan, with 32 specific cost-cutting suggestions, is called *How To Save £50 Billion*, though in fact the savings in the first year would be only £42.5 billion. (I say *only* £42.5 billion — which shows the scale of the problem.) Only by freezing civil service salaries for two years running would the savings reach £50 billion.

The biggest saving, accounting for more than £10 billion of the total, would come from radical cuts in state benefits to the middle classes — abolishing child benefit and the child trust fund, but raising the child tax credit to ensure poorer families are no worse off. Subsidised student loans, free bus passes and free TV licences for the elderly would go, but again, poorer people would be compensated. The welfare system would be targeted more on the poor, and be much less of a middle-class scam. About time too.

Other savings come from cutting programmes that just do not work, such as Sure Start, Building Schools for the Future (all government programmes, however useless, have upbeat names) and the Education Maintenance Allowance. Government advertising would be halved, ID cards abandoned, and the school leaving age would not be raised to 18. Less would go on consultants, on the administration of health and education, and on regional government. Instead of expanding overseas aid as the Conservatives intend, the department's budget would be frozen, as would those of others.

A useful saving of £2 billion would come from making civil servants contribute one-third more towards their gold-plated pension schemes. And a massive £6 billion would come from a one-year pay freeze across the public sector, with the exception of soldiers in the field. That could become a two-year freeze if the dire economic circumstances demanded it.

How to save £150 billion

Nice try: but frankly, we need to trim public spending not by £50 billion, but more like £150 billion — roughly a quarter, in other words — to have much hope of keeping ourselves out of bankruptcy. Does that seem a lot? It is not really so much. The state has grown by about half since 1997, so it does no more than pare back just half the *increase* in spending during the Blair-Brown years. Does anyone really think that all that extra spending has been so absolutely essential that we could not possibly live without all of it?

Instead of starting from where we are now, and trying forlornly to find 'efficiency savings', we should start instead with a blank sheet of paper and ask what it is that we want government to do. There are some obligations such as pensions and welfare spending (say, £225 billion a year), and let us for the moment accept that health spending (over £100 billion) should escape any cuts. A money-follows-the-child school system (which I will outline later) could provide a £4,700 education for every kid at a cost of just £60 billion a year. Maintain spending on transport (£30 billion) and other core functions such as justice, defence, and foreign policy (£80 billion) and even £30 billion of debt interest payments, and you reach £525 billion — just over £150 billion less than the projected 2009/10 total, even before we start looking for 'efficiencies'. Does government really need to do more than all that?

The Canadian therapy

Across-the-board cuts in budgets and one-year freezes in salaries and benefits might well give temporary breathing space to government bookkeepers and concentrate civil service minds. The public would love it, too. But it is no long-term way to balance budgets. Many state employees are low paid (though, after the noughties spending explosion, fewer of them than before) and freezes would hurt them disproportionately — hence David Cameron's promise to exclude them from any such measure.

Furthermore, focusing on spending targets for each ministry simply creates antagonism and disunity between spending ministers and Treasury ministers. At best, the departments simply spend up to the centrally imposed limits, rather than looking critically at what they deliver and how they deliver it. At worst, the antagonism spills over into public arguments, with spending ministers briefing against the Treasury and trying to recruit public support to preserve their empires.

When Canada in the late 1980s and early 1990s attempted to reduce a ballooning public deficit through cuts and pay freezes, morale among public service providers slumped, and the country was hit by strikes. Since the services that people valued were cut just as severely as those that nobody would have missed, citizens' trust in the government and public sector was destroyed. As for 'efficiency' programmes to 'cut waste' — well, the Canadian experience is that they help, but do not actually achieve major cuts in costs.

The incoming Liberal government of 1993 faced public debt approaching 70% of GDP, roughly the level forecast for the UK in 2011/12. Yet they managed to reduce annual borrowing from 9.1% of GDP to zero in just five years — with budget surpluses nearly every year since — almost exclusively by cutting spending. Between 1993 and 1997, spending fell by 9% of GDP, while taxes hardly rose at all. Not surprisingly, when Jocelyn Bourgon, the confident head of Canada's civil service at the time, came to London in 2009 to explain how they did it, the Conservatives bought ringside seats — and hastily arranged private interviews afterwards. They believe that the Canadian experience can provide a model for turning round the UK's huge debt juggernaut.

How did the Canadians manage it? Their first move was to appoint a minister with the specific responsibility for public service renewal, so that there was a single, senior person with the authority to drive through the change process and make sure every other minister did their bit. They rejected across-the-board cuts and freezes, but nothing else was off limits. There were not even central spending targets — the government knew that the centre could not second-guess what different ministries actually needed, and that departments would simply spend up to whatever targets were set, instead of making economies.

Otherwise, every part of the public service would be under scrutiny, with no exceptions and exclusions — not even healthcare or foreign aid. There would be a complete review of all areas of government activity. Ministers were each charged with defining what their department was there to do. What was their core purpose? Did it really need civil servants to achieve it, or could it be done better, cheaper, and more efficiently by private providers or by the public themselves? With one high-ranking reform minister in charge, there could be no stonewalling or hiding from such tough decisions. And with a *reform* rather than a *finance* minister in charge, everyone accepted that this was an exercise in completely reshaping, modernising and rethinking the government's engagement with citizens — not just an exercise in penny-pinching.

The pressure was kept up through cabinet retreats at which ministers' progress would be scored and new targets set. On this subject, everyone knew that the prime minister, the finance minister and everyone else had to speak with one voice, and there could be none of the departmental jostling that we see in the UK's annual spending rounds. Meanwhile, a co-ordinating panel of ministers built up expertise that could be focused on the reformation of one department after another.

The process recognised that some public service functions remained vital, while others could be completely redesigned or even eliminated. The end result was small cuts (or even increases) in some departments, but large savings in others whose role was redefined — massive cuts in transport and farm subsidies, for example, but rises in benefits for the elderly.

Within three years, Canada's budget deficits were eliminated and the debt started to come down. Within five years, the size of the civil service had fallen by nearly a quarter (23%) — all with no strikes or civil unrest. Before long, with the economy returning to health, the government budget could actually start growing again.

Today, with the UK government bloated and out of shape from years of overspending and initiativitis, the Canadian strategy seems exactly the right model for the UK to follow. Our government too should appoint a senior minister for public sector renewal, and conduct a complete review of what it does, what it needs to do, how to do that better, and what is best left to other people. Focus on that, and the savings will come anyway.

Signing the pledge

Georgia — the East European republic, not the American state — might seem both far away and very different from either the UK or Canada, but it too managed to revive a debt-ridden and failing economy in no time flat. Much of that was down to the shrewd policies of Vladimer 'Lado' Gurgenidze, the charismatic head of the central bank between 2004 and

2007, and then Prime Minister for a year after that. An inspirational speaker and now an international businessman, he comes often to the UK and is always delighted to explain how Georgia's GDP per head nearly tripled between 2004 and 2008, with year-on-year economic growth averaging 7.8%. It even grew in the credit-crunch year of 2008, when the UK economy contracted.

So proud are the Georgians of their success that in October 2009 the president, Mikheil Saakashvilli, introduced a proposal to enshrine Georgia's sound economic management techniques into the constitution. The measures would cap government expenditure at 30% of GDP (the UK's is half as much again, at 44%) and the budget deficit at 3% of GDP (ours is 12.4%). The national debt will be capped at 60% of GDP (a level through which ours will soar quite soon). The Georgian proposals also specifically outlaw the sort of sleight-of-hand by which five-sixths of the UK's public debt does not show in the government's books.

Another key part of the measures is that the spending and borrowing limits must be met over fixed 3–5 year periods. Gordon Brown, when Chancellor, of course, had his own 'golden rule' that the government should borrow only to invest, and should maintain sound finances over the economic cycle. Unfortunately the terms 'invest' and 'cycle' seemed capable of infinite stretching as the Treasury's need arose — until at last, under the strain of the bank bailouts, the elastic broke completely.

As Douglas Carswell pointed out, public spending and borrowing are hard to restrain. Adopting rules to keep them in check seems entirely 'prudent', as one former Chancellor would say. It is a sound policy for government. But the rules should be strictly defined, making the government meet its policy over, say, four years, the lifetime of a parliament. So when voters go to the polls, they can look at the figures and judge how 'prudently' their politicians have managed their money.

I hate quangos and would close all of them down tomorrow, but I can see a case for having bodies that restrain our leaders' financial alcoholism. So, just as we have a Monetary Policy Committee (MPC) to prevent politicians taking liberties with our currency, so should we have a Fiscal Policy Committee (FPC) to prevent them taking liberties with the public budget. An independent body, it would ensure that government liabilities were properly disclosed, and force spending limits if the debt and borrowing rules were breached. It would act rather like the OECD or the IMF does right now — except that when it warned of overspending and overborrowing, profligate politicians could not simply ignore it.

3

REFORM OF THE FINANCIAL SYSTEM

THE *REAL* MERCHANT BANKERS WHO CAUSED THE CRISIS

Of course, if you believe the politicians, it is not them but bankers who are to blame for this mess in the first place. As a display of buck-passing, it sure beats the Chicago Cardinals.

The truth is that in the decade to 2007, the Bank of England — pushed by the politicians and emboldened by fact that much the same was happening in the United States — created a fake boom by printing too much money and making credit far too cheap. Meanwhile, Gordon Brown's new bank regulator, the Financial Services Authority (FSA) seemed more interested in creating rules on how quickly the banks picked up the phone to their customers, than in the fundamental security of the banking system. But then it was very much more distant from the day-to-day workings of the financial market than the Bank of England regulators whom it replaced: they, at least, could see who was coming into Threadneedle Street to borrow money, and a quiver of the Governor's eyebrows could make them pull back from excessive risk.

So now the bankers found themselves at a poker table, where the government was handing out free gaming chips and the regulators were buying drinks at the bar. Not surprisingly, they took full advantage and gambled away, making some very risky bets that they would not normally have entertained.

Our long history of fiscal alcoholism

The politicians started their cheap money habit back in the 1980s. President Jimmy Carter's Community Reinvestment Act forced American lenders to give home loans to poor minorities with poor credit ratings. The intention, to give them a chance of getting onto the housing ladder, was admirable: but for the banks and Savings & Loan (S&L) institutions, it was very bad business. In 1985, a number of them failed and there were government-forced mergers. In October 1987, the US and UK stock markets collapsed, fearing a reprise. In response, the Federal Reserve Chairman Alan Greenspan in Washington and Chancellor Nigel Lawson in London agreed to flood the world with cash. It worked: the markets rose again and business picked itself up and carried on. The officials and the politicians congratulated themselves that they had put an end to boom and bust.

In reality, however, they had put a temporary end to bust only by creating an artificial, and ultimately explosive, boom. At every passing crisis, they stoked it further by throwing still more money at the markets — such as when the stock markets crashed in 1987, or Russia reneged on its debts in 1998, and most spectacularly, after the shock of 9/11, when US interest rates were slashed from over 6% to just 1% — whereupon families rushed to take out cheap mortgages, and house prices soared. Bankers, deal-makers, and home buyers had never had it so good — so they thought.

Even with house prices going crazy, and the pound

through the roof, the Bank of England's Monetary Policy Committee (MPC) seemed unaware how much it was over-fuelling the economy. Gordon Brown said it had to focus entirely on the Consumer Price Index (CPI) — which, conveniently for him, ignored those spiralling housing costs. The MPC also failed see that all those cheap clothes, electronics and toys that China was dumping on us should have sent the CPI *falling*, not rising at the Bank's 2% annual target. So the over-fuelling continued.

Nor did the FSA notice the explosion that was looming, although it was written all over the banks' accounts. Indeed, even at the very height of the boom, they were promoting the new Basel II regulations, which eased the amount of hard cash that banks had to keep in their vaults just in case of problems. Bank shareholders and executives naturally concluded that what was OK for the regulator was OK for them; so they went out and lent even more, and found all sorts of new ways to make even more risky bets. Of course, the government — which needed to borrow increasingly vast amounts to finance its ambitious spending plans — was one of their best customers.

Given such incompetence from the monetary and regulatory authorities, and the connivance of a big-spending, big-borrowing government, it really is a bit much for Gordon Brown and his colleagues to say that the ensuing crisis was all down to greedy bankers and had nothing to do with them.

The 2007 crisis

The crisis came in 2007, when the MPC realised that interest rates were far too low, and raised them — far too quickly. With much less credit around, banks began to run out of cash for their day-to-day operations, but still the MPC kept interest rates high. Even after the failure of Northern Rock, which exposed the banks' cash-flow problem, they kept interest rates high. A year later, predictably, the giant-size banks HBOS and RBS hit the buffers, and the rest is (a very expensive) history.

Bad American mortgage loans certainly did infect our banking system; but it was inept UK policy that brought it to its deathbed. A less reckless monetary policy, a little temporary Bank of England 'last resort' lending when it was needed back in 2007, and regulators who actually understood the banks' risk-taking, would have averted the whole catastrophe.

Taxpayers now own 84% of RBS and 43% of Lloyds/HBOS. The irony is that we are now at risk for far bigger sums than would have been needed to avert the crisis in the first place. Taxpayers are standing guarantee for £2 trillion worth of RBS assets and liabilities (though nobody is quite sure how much of their book is an asset and how much is a liability), and another £1 trillion worth in the case of Lloyds/HBOS. Yes, that is £3 *trillion*, twice the nation's yearly income, and five times what the government pulls in annually through taxation.

Back in 2007, the Bank of England should have seen that its hike in interest rates was causing problems — or more accurately, was exposing the problems that had built up under its low-interest rate policy — and made 'last resort' loans to the banks. The regulator should then have forced the banks to curb their risks, cut their costs, slice boardroom salaries, and get back into competitive shape. Instead, the government reduced competition even further by forcing the 'bad' bank HBOS to merge with the 'good' bank Lloyds — creating a group in which the good bits were irredeemably tainted by the bad.

Scrabbling to pick up the pieces

The next part of this agony in three fits saw the government scrabbling to find the cash to pay for the disastrous situation it had got us into. Economists advised that more money had to be printed in order to re-float our cash-starved financial system. Others thought that printing money would just devalue the stuff even further and lead to rising prices. For my own part (wherever you have two economists you get three points of view), I thought that the punk monetarists were right and that business needed a fresh injection of new money — provided that the Bank would be brave enough to take the needle out again when things started to improve: which on past experience, would require a certain optimism.

Sadly, the only people to get any benefit from all this new cash were the government. Here is how it worked. In 2009 the Bank of England set about printing £175 billion worth of new money — trebling the amount of the stuff in circulation. The Bank used that to buy government bonds. Ordinarily, that means the government would have £175 billion extra to hand out in benefits and salaries. But of course in 2009 that £175 billion exactly matched, as if by magic, the amount that the government reckoned it needed to borrow to keep afloat. (When it became clear that £175 billion was not enough to feed the government's overspending habit, the Bank of England kindly agreed to print another £25 billion of new money to keep the party going.)

In other words, the Bank of England's cash simply bailed out the government: none of it actually got to the cash-starved individuals and businesses in the private sector. Even worse, the government told the banks that they had been so reckless that from now on, they would have to hold a lot more solid securities in their vaults — *government* securities, of course. So now the banks find themselves having to buy government bonds, rather than lending to their customers. It is no wonder that so many UK businesses failed and that our recession was deeper and longer than those of other developed countries.

A few kind words about bankers

Few people understand that the root cause of our economic problems is inept and self-indulgent government policy. They blame only the banks, which — after huge taxpayer bailouts — are refusing them loans and repossessing their homes. Now we have the unseemly spectacle of politicians of all sides courting the votes of everyone who thinks it is the banks that have let them down.

In particular, the enormous bonuses paid to some bank executives have come in for a pasting. Now I happen to think that bankers have paid themselves far too much for what they do — though providing insurance, finance, and capital to UK trade and industry is indeed an important function, and far from 'socially useless' as Lord Turner, head of the failed financial regulator, put it. (Not that anyone made much of a fuss about the £33 million in bonuses that the socially useless FSA quietly paid its staff in 2009.)

The bankers paid themselves too much for two reasons. Firstly, from 2003 until the crash, those heady days when you could pluck tenners off the trees, business was booming: every deal worked, so people were incentivised with fat bonuses to do more deals. Sure, lots of those deals unwound after the crunch, but few people anticipated that. Meanwhile, paying fat bonuses was just good business. But again, the root of that fantasyland finance was government policy.

Secondly, there was — and is — just far too little competition in banking. Wave upon wave of bureaucratic regulation has loaded more and more cost onto financial services firms. They need to be enormous simply to afford the vast compliance teams they need to fill in all the forms produced by 2,700 FSA civil servants. So fewer new ones ever get started.

Governments make poor bankers

So now, the same people who brought you the General Practitioners' contract — £100,000 a year, no weekend or evening work, bonus payments for what you do anyway, and a lot more time free for the golf course — are going to be second-guessing bank staff contracts too. If the media are complaining that bonuses are too high, they can strike them down. If they think a contract rewards risk-taking too much, they can tear it up. If they feel customer charges are too high, they will intervene.

It is not obvious how bank executives can run their business when career politicians who know nothing it are rewriting any board minute, every contract, any decisions, any wage negotiations, or any business deals that they fear might bring them a bad press. Talented staff will simply up sticks and go to Switzerland or any of the other financial centres where they do not get so messed around; talented executives will give up the idea of a career in banking and go to some other sector where they are not bullied as much.

Yet as long as politicians own large chunks of our banks, the public and the media will be pushing them to micro-manage the financial sector. In such a highly competitive and mobile world, that will be a true disaster for the UK.

And face it: the government does not understand the finance industry. In 2008 the Treasury gave the Royal Bank of Scotland a clean bill of health; just a week later, it had to bail it out with £37 billion. According to the National Audit Office, the government spent a total of £117 billion buying bank shares or lending to financial institutions — roughly £5,500 per family. Its total support for them has reached a staggering £850 billion, about £40,000 per family. And another £107 million was paid to City lawyers and advisers because the Treasury was 'too stretched' to cope with the crisis that it failed to foresee.

Getting politicians out of banking

A priority for politicians, then, is to get out of banking, and unwind the taxpayers' guarantee of bank assets, as fast as they can. But there is a lot to put right before that can happen. If taxpayers are to get at least some value back, the banks have to be turned into strong, competitive enterprises in a strong, competitive financial market.

That may not be easy. For most of 2008-09, the banks cashed in on cheap loans from the Bank of England: they have kept afloat by taking cheap cash from the government, and lending it out at a profit. Now it is payback time: the cheap loans have gone, and outstanding ones have to be repaid soon, which means the banks will face an extra £6 billion of higher interest costs over 2010-14. UK banks are going to struggle. It is hard to imagine that the government's involvement in them will be purely temporary.

A few frank words about regulators

A lot of people — including of course the regulators — say that we need more regulation on the banks. Various EU governments have called for more international regulation. Well they would, wouldn't they?

We do not need more regulation on banks. Tighter regulation will just force institutions to seek out sneakier and sneakier ways of escaping it — encouraging the growth of an unregulated 'shadow banking' sector. No, we need *less* regulation — less rulebook micro-management, and more targeted supervision of the banks' exposure to risk. In fact, we should relax the controls on the banks' capital structure when there is a downturn — like now — and tighten them as things improve. The regulators did exactly the opposite.

The FSA, which failed at its first hurdle, is plainly not up to this. George Osborne said he would turn it into a consumer champion, but it is too bloated to be of any use for anything, and its culture and practices are all wrong. Instead, like Carthage, its buildings should be razed to the ground, no stone left upon another, and salt strewn on the foundations so that nothing might grow there again.

The only other possible regulator is the Bank of England, which is in a good position to supervise banks, since it is active in the same markets and knows what is going on. (It warned the FSA months before the Northern Rock debacle, but apart from a quick phone call to the Rock's chairman, the FSA took no action.) Indeed, it used to regulate the banks: it did not stave off every failure (remember BCCI), but at least it averted a widespread banking disaster, which is more than the FSA did.

While the Bank of England is undoubtedly the best body to regulate the banks — though it would have to rebuild that expertise, which was scattered to the four winds by Gordon Brown in 1997 — its Monetary Policy Committee has plainly failed to set interest rates properly. It is still better than having Chancellors of the Exchequer setting rates, because then you get political interests tainting every decision, like the need to make everyone feel good before by-elections. But the MPC's hot and cold bath technique gave us all financial flu. No official should set interest rates: interest rates are the price of borrowing, and like any other price, the market should set them. Sure, the market will not always get the price right; but with so many shrewd financial players out there, markets are likely to make a better job of it than a bunch of academics and quangocrats.

We certainly do *not* want some new supra-national regulator, such as the EU has proposed, messing up our financial sector. London is the only real international market in the EU: it has more to gain or lose from running a successful market than everyone else put together, so it really should be sorting out its own problems. If EU regulators gum up London, the whole of the EU is the loser, and there are plenty of people in the US and Switzerland who will rub their hands with glee at Europe's self-bondage.

Yet there are plenty of folk in Paris and Berlin who are jealous of the UK's dominance and would love to curb it. How could we trust any regulation from such a source? (The head of the IMF, the French socialist Dominique Strauss-Kahn, plans new bank taxes and for the UK to lose its seat at the IMF top table. No hint of nationalism there, then.) In any event, this crisis did not occur because of any lack of *international* regulation — indeed the Basel II regulations made it worse. The crisis was down to failures in individual countries, like ours.

The banks are certainly not going to recover if we start slapping pointless taxes on them. The tax enthusiasts say that governments would squirrel away this tax money until the next financial crisis, when they would return it to the banks. Anyone who knows anything about politicians and money can see that this is barmy. In March 2009 the FSA suggested that the banks themselves should be forced to hide away cash as a bolster against future crises — the very sort of fantasy bookkeeping that in past times the FSA was complaining about. Secret bank reserves were outlawed forty years ago, and rightly so.

A lot of fuss has been made about the role of hedge funds. It is easy for politicians and regulators to blame them, because no ordinary person has the foggiest idea what a hedge fund is or does. Well, in fact there are about 10,000 of them, and they invest the money of private clients, all large and savvy investors, who probably know far more about the state of the markets than any pen pusher at the FSA. They actually take less risk than the banks did: before the crisis, when the banks were lending eight times more than the cash, IOUs and other assets they had in their vaults, the hedge funds were liable for only three times, and they have become even more cautious now. So they are hardly reckless. Yes, they do short-sell basket cases such as Northern Rock, precipitating their decline. But that is because they have expert knowledge of what is actually happening in that particular market. They do not *cause* the problems which Northern Rock and others get themselves into; their selling simply *exposes* the risks and problems that already exist but which like half-blind regulators have not picked up on.

Breaking up the state banks

It is up to the UK government to fix the financial sector, starting with the huge banks that they own. Those leviathans need to shed cost and complacency. They must be made more competitive, which means splitting them up and creating perhaps five or six UK clearing banks, or more: when small banks fail, the rest of us can survive, but when banks the size of RBS or HBOS fail, we cannot. Yes, the banks need to be stress tested: but the key test is what happens to the whole economy in the event of a bank failure, not the distress of the bank itself.

To make smaller banks viable and able to take the stress of modern financial markets, however, means that the regulatory burden has to be lightened, even while its is being sharpened to focus on the fundamentals that really matter. Smaller banks should have less onerous reserve requirements than larger ones. We need to make sure that larger banks are as safe as we can make them, within the realities of the banking business and the need for all businesses to take risks in order to progress and develop. The failure of huge banks, as we have seen, is not just a problem for them and their customers, but a problem for the entire financial system. We can recover much more easily from the failure of a smaller bank: so the regulation on smaller banks can be lighter.

A lighter regulatory burden means lower start-up costs for new banking groups, which has the happy consequence of promoting competition still further. Lighter, better regulation would also strengthen the whole financial market, boosting the value of our nationalised banks and making it much easier to return them to the private sector when the time comes, as before long it must.

Meanwhile, the government urgently needs to reduce its borrowing. With all the extra money that the Bank of England is printing — another £25 billion of it in early 2010 — being sucked up by the government to fuel its spending, there is nothing left over to lubricate the wheels of business, and therefore of economic recovery. For a long time, politicians have been telling us that cutting back public spending (or, as they put it, 'investment') now would choke off any recovery. The exact opposite is true. It is the amount of money that the government has been spending and borrowing that has left the productive side of the economy starved of the cash it needs to survive and expand. It would be nice if our politicians were big enough to admit that, and to do something about it.

4

POLITICIANS

MAKING THEM GET IT

In 1990, scientists from North Carolina reported having found traces of the toxic substance benzene in bottles of Perrier, the sparkling mineral water that comes from a spring in Vergèze in southern France. Journalists immediately asked Perrier what they were going to do, but the company was not sure. The product was still safe to drink, and few consignments seemed affected.

But Perrier's problem was that this was not just about the safety of its water. It was about the public's trust in its brand. Perrier's entire marketing strategy was to sell itself on the purity of its product — and plainly, the product was not 'pure'.

Perrier had little option but to withdraw 160 million bottles of the product worldwide. But its messages were mixed. It ventured various explanations for the benzene contamination, eventually explaining that it was due to a worker making a mistake in the filtering process, and that the spring itself remained unpolluted. In the meantime the parent company Source Perrier gave scant guidance to its worldwide subsidiaries, whose statements were inconsistent, further fuelling people's worries about the product. In brand terms, it was a disaster. The public's trust in Perrier was shattered. There was none on the shelves for four months. Rivals made hay. Groupe Perrier struggled. In 1992 it was taken over by Nestlé, jobs were cut and a large loss was recorded. While it is now back and happily providing pure fizz to millions of thirsty people in nearly every country, Perrier has never returned to its pre-1990 dominance of the sparkling water market.

Westminster's polluted brand

Public affairs practitioners use the Perrier case as an example of how not just a product, but a worldwide brand, can be polluted when a company does not act decisively in a crisis. Given the almost daily round of champagne-swilling and canapé-guzzling Westminster receptions that public affairs companies throw for Members of Parliament and at which the two groups exchange views and pleasantries, you might have thought that MPs would have been more aware of the need to protect their own 'brand'.

Not a bit of it, though. When someone made a Freedom of Information (FoI) request for information on MPs' expenses, the first response of the House of Commons, led by Speaker Michael Martin, was to try to block the request in court. Indeed, Speaker Martin spent £100,000 of taxpayers' money on a High Court case that Parliament's lawyers said he could not win, trying to prevent taxpayers finding out what MPs had been claiming. He complained that the publication of MPs' receipts would reveal their home addresses and so put them at risk of attack from crazies (or more likely, disgruntled members of the taxpaying public). The court rejected this, whereupon the Commons agreed to publish the information, but the 'sensitive information' would be 'redacted' — a courtly way of saying 'blacked out'.

But the *Daily Telegraph* got its hands on the expenses files, and although it was careful about concealing telephone numbers, precise addresses and other sensitive items, it was good for democracy that it did. Because the 'redacted' version — which Parliament clunkily published anyway — would have prevented anyone seeing the true extent to which MPs were playing the system in order to maximize their allowances on their second homes.

Parliament's perks

It is not unreasonable that MPs who live out of London should be given some contribution towards having a second home in the capital. They often work long hours — less than they did before the 'family friendly' hours that brought an end to midnight and early-hours sittings, but still there are all those receptions, dinners and other social engagements to go to. Many taxpayers might regard these as just free booze-ups, but in reality, much of an MP's work is done at these networking events. The expenses system reflected this, allowing them to claim for a second home.

Yet the rules were much less clear about what a 'second' home was. Many MPs worked out that if they designated their family home in the constituency as their 'second' home, they could get expenses for far larger running costs than they would by claiming on some small London flat. Many others discovered that by 'flipping' — first designating their constituency home, then their London flat, as their 'second' home, they could do some nice subsidised re-furnishing and redecoration in both. Or you could get the taxpayer to decorate your dilapidated old flat, then flog it off at a profit, and then do the same again. And you could tell the House of

Commons that one home was your second home, and Customs & Revenue that it was your main residence, pulling in all the expenses to run it, but avoiding capital gains tax when you sold it. Nice.

MPs claimed around £33 million in expenses in 2008/09, and of course enjoyed all those free dinners, subsidised food and drink in Westminster, and fact-finding trips round the world. Speaker Martin himself provided his wife with £4,000 worth of taxi trips, by no means all of them on official business. Generous to a fault — the fault being that taxpayers footed her bills.

The storm of public protest at the scams that the *Daily Telegraph* revealed was unprecedented. The reputation of MPs was never so low. Not that it was ever high: it had already been undermined by years of 'good day to bury bad news' spin that left people wondering if they could believe anything ministers told them. Then there was the lavish lifestyles — John Prescott playing croquet at his 21-room country retreat, the Lord Chancellor's £650,000 free makeover of his official flat and his £1,900,000 pension, Peter Mandelson's £373,000 loan from fellow minister Geoffrey Robinson…the tarnish was everywhere.

The need for honest rules

The most remarkable thing, though, was how MPs sincerely believed they had nothing to apologise for. They said they were simply following the rules laid down by the parliamentary Fees Office, which is in charge of MPs' pay and expenses. Why should they be vilified for that?

I know many MPs and most of them really do think the vituperation against them is completely unfair. Sometimes it is. Douglas Hogg, for example, was forced out by party leader David Cameron after allegedly claiming £2,115 expenses for cleaning out the moat of his mediaeval manor house. In fact, Hogg explained, he had simply handed the Fees Office all the running costs of his home (including £18,000 for a gardener and £671 for a mole-catcher), and asked them to sort out which he could and could not claim. But the Conservatives' rule is that it is fine to be a toff provided you do not act like one, so he had to go.

What too many MPs have not been able to 'get', though, is that the public regards the rules themselves as dishonest — so the fact that you acted within them is no defence against charges of dishonesty. In fact, the rules were a fraud from the start. There is never a good time for MPs to raise their own wages, so in the 1980s they cooked up a new expenses system. At least, it was called 'expenses', but everyone knew it was really a disguised pay rise. The deal was that expense claims would remain confidential, so MPs (with the connivance of the whips and of the Fees Office) knew they could be liberal with them. The Freedom of Information Act, however, shattered that confidentiality. The rest you know.

A system with no room for fiddling

This rotten system must go. But MPs do need some help towards London living — we do not want Parliament to become the preserve only for people rich enough to afford their own Westminster flat. A sensible alternative might be to abolish MPs' home expenses entirely, but raise their pay to compensate for reasonable living costs — though the public think that pay rises would be a cheek, given what MPs have done. Another option is to provide London accommodation to those who need it. After all, the parliamentary week is short — most MPs return to their constituencies on a

Thursday evening — so it hardly needs to be lavish. There are plenty of buildings around Westminster that could be converted into hotel-style accommodation. London's universities, and some companies, maintain flats and bedsits in the capital for their personnel — why cannot Parliament do the same?

What expenses MPs do claim, travel costs for example, should *all* be completely open and transparent. They are best published online in a format that anyone could access. The thought that newspapers and opponents would know exactly what is being claimed would encourage thrift and honesty.

There is also the issue of MPs hiring their own family members. Many MPs employ their partners as personal assistants, which makes perfect sense: a partner will understand the constituency, and fit in with the MP's unusual hours and engagements. Then again, some MPs inflate their family income by hiring relatives, at taxpayers' expense, in return for very little work. Once more, public trust has been broken. As those public affairs people will tell you, trust is something that takes a lot of pain, time and effort to rebuild. So there is really no option: MPs must be banned from employing family members, either their own or those of any other MP. That may seem unfair to the majority who believe that hiring partners is efficient and no abuse of the system, but it is the only way of rebuilding the public's trust in MPs.

As Douglas Carswell and the charismatic MEP Daniel Hannan — whose 'devalued prime minister' attack on Gordon Brown has topped 2,500,000 hits on YouTube — say in their excellent 2008 book *The Plan*, MPs should also have to live by the same rules they force on the rest of us. It might be good to get more women in Parliament, but when sex discrimination is illegal for us, how come political parties are allowed all-women shortlists? Why should Parliament think itself exempt from Freedom of Information requests? Why can ministers enjoy pensions that are far bigger than those allowed to the rest of us? Why can you smoke in Westminster's bars, but not in any other pub or club in the UK?

A hairshirt regime on expenses, salaries, staff and rules might irritate the more long-standing and honest MPs, though probably not to the many hundreds in the 2010 new intake. But Parliament must regain our confidence, because it has a vital job to do — one it is not doing at the moment. Parliament emerged, eight hundred years ago, to debate and represent the views of the public, and to protect us against the unrestrained power of the executive — in those days, the king, and these days, the prime minister and the ruling party.

The sociology of Parliament

Just as Andrew Lilico is an economist's economist, so his boss Neil O'Brien, the head of Policy Exchange, is a think-tanker's think-tanker. He thinks at five hundred words a minute and these thoughts emerge at about three hundred. Any topic you care to mention, he has pondered and has ideas on. He doesn't always know the answer, but he generally knows at least six different options, and can tell you how they have worked or failed in twelve different countries.

'Parliament is simply not functional,' he says. 'It's not fit for purpose.' He thinks it should be restraining government ministers, holding them to account, and making sure that policy reflects the views of the public and of justice, rather than the interests of the political class. To achieve that, we need 'a cap on executive numbers,' he suggests. 'Or separation of powers.'

What he means is that of the 635 seats in Parliament today, 120 are occupied by ministers and other party hacks on the government payroll. They owe their careers, salaries and pensions to the prime minister and the party bosses, so naturally they are inclined to vote for whatever Downing Street tells them to. Indeed, to vote against them on anything, however small, would be a resigning issue. And there are yet more MPs who would dearly *love* to be on the payroll, plus many more who live in fear of the whips, or of being deselected as candidates, if they rock the boat. So roughly half the House of Commons are not there representing the people at all — they vote as the 'executive' dictates.

One simple thought, suggests O'Brien (as I say, he has plenty) would be to cap the number of ministers. As Carswell and Hannan point out, we fought the Second World War with only 75 ministers: do we really need more than sixty or so now? But would that actually make much of a difference, when the party whips remain so powerful? Perhaps not.

The more radical option would be to separate the executive from Parliament entirely, so that — American-style — ministers did not sit in the House of Commons at all. I favour this as the only long-term solution. But it is so different from what we have now, and from our parliamentary tradition, that it could be very difficult to engineer.

The constitutional monarchy

If we are not going to boot ministers out of Parliament so that the Lords and the Commons can do a proper job of holding the executive to account, then we need mechanisms to restrain them. Having an executive that through force of numbers and patronage can control the legislative sovereignty of Parliament is a very dangerous setup. Already we see the injustices that such an all-powerful government is capable of.

I am sad to say it, but in this context the Queen has been absolutely pathetic, and has badly let us down. The reason why we have traditionally rubbed along with monarchs being officially head of the government — and head of the church, the justice system, the peerage and the armed forces — is not for the power that they wield but the power that they deny politicians. For most of the time, our monarchs have been far more in tune with the mood of their people, and have had a far more acute grasp of their rights and freedoms, than have ministers: so this has proved a useful arrangement.

The royal family does not want to get involved in party politics. Yet if the Queen is not going to stop politicians from usurping power and turning themselves into an elected dictatorship, who is? With Magna Carta, the Queen's distant ancestor agreed to fundamental principles such as our right not to be held without trial, and to be tried by a jury. Yet in her own reign (starting perhaps in 1971 with internment in Northern Ireland, but escalating fast in the last dozen years) these rights, and more, have simply been signed away.

The constitutional role of an unelected, hereditary monarchy must be limited. But it *does* have a constitutional role, and *must* exercise that role as a necessary counterweight to the otherwise unbridled power of an executive that effectively controls Parliament. It is time for both Palace and Parliament to initiate a genuine public debate on that role, and on when and how the monarchy should legitimately intervene to ensure that the rights and civil liberties of the people are preserved.

Reforming the business of Parliament

Of course, there are interim fixes that might help a bit. Speaker John Bercow wants to limit the ruling party's control of the parliamentary timetable. Others have suggested fixed election terms of four years so that prime ministers lose the power to call elections on the back of favourable polls, rather than when it is right for the country. Carswell and Hannan would like to see the heads of Commons committees — which can question ministers and hold them to account — elected by MPs rather than chosen by the whips, which they say would give committees much more independence. (I would like to see committee chairs chosen from opposition MPs, giving the government even less sway over them.) Carswell and Hannan would also let MPs question civil servants and quango bosses (again, I would say that quangos and regulators should report directly to Parliament rather than to ministers). Parliamentary committees, they argue, should hold hearings with candidates for important public jobs — like judges and quango chiefs — and scrutinise the annual budgets of Whitehall departments. Parliament, not ministers, would have control over which foreign treaties the UK signs up to.

Other people, though, are thinking through the role of Parliament afresh — like Iain Dale. Just as Andrew Lilico is an economist's economist and Neil O'Brien is a think-tanker's think-tanker, so Iain Dale is a blogger's blogger. A big man (though slightly slimmer these days after a sponsored diet) with a big personality, he is prolific on all the social networking sites and on his own blog, Iain Dale's diary, which has an enormous following. He talks with one eye on me and one on his laptop, from which he is constantly moderating blog comments or jotting down ideas for new pieces.

'We need to give Parliament back its power as the representative voice for the people,' he says. 'The executive branch — ministers and Downing Street — should be an agent of Parliament, not the other way round. That is really crucial. We need to ask what the central purpose of Parliament is. And it is to represent the people, not to rubber-stamp the political wish-list of the ruling party.'

'Parliament must get much closer to the people,' he continues. He would like to see the House of Commons regularly debating the top proposals (the 'early day motions') introduced by backbench MPs — ideas which often reflect pressing public concerns but which today are routinely kicked into the long grass by the government whips. Likewise, Dale would like to see MPs debate the most popular petitions that are posted by the public on the Downing Street website. As a prolific blogger he would — of course — like to see Parliament conducting online consultations and polls, and debating the results.

Party leaders have found it convenient to clamp down on their MPs having outside jobs. It looks bad when someone is taking home a salary of £64,766 (plus office and staff costs, travel and second home allowances) for supposedly being a full-time MP, and then pockets more for being a part-time company director, or lawyer or consultant. In fact, it would be better if MPs *did* have outside jobs, and if being an MP was seen as a less than full-time occupation. They might then have at least some idea of how to run organisations, and of the many problems facing ordinary people and their businesses.

At a more mechanical level, the guillotine, used to curtail debates that the government is fed up with — which has been used more in the last five years than in the last fifty — should be reformed so that it could only be used in the most extreme circumstances, enabling real debate to happen. And there is common agreement that the power of the party whips should be curbed — not that anyone has much idea how to do it.

How Parliament can find the plot again

In a paper for the Adam Smith Institute published on 5 November 2009 and impishly entitled *Knaves and Fawkes*, Tim Ambler and Keith Boyfield argue that the way Parliament uses its time needs radical change, to reflect the concerns of the general public and the importance of the legislation under discussion. Over 80% of voters, they say, think that Parliament just does not work. It has nothing to do with the expenses scandal: Parliament has simply 'lost the plot'. Today, while much of MPs' time is occupied discussing trivial items like road works, important items like the EU Lisbon treaty are hardly discussed at all. (The UK went to war in Iraq with only seven hours of debate. The foxhunting ban got seven hundred hours.)

Some 3,500 new 'statutory instrument' regulations go through Parliament each year. That is about 20 for every day Parliament sits, far too many for MPs to read, never mind debate — and indeed, they are never debated at all. Many, of course, are extremely minor administrative wording changes. But others are important amendments to the law, such as when in October 2009 the government greatly extended the powers of various agencies to enter people's homes under the Proceeds of Crime Act and seize their assets if they are suspected of profiting through crime. That is the sort of thing that eventually ends up like the American system, where someone accused — not *convicted* — of crime can see all their assets frozen, and so be unable to pay for any defence.

You may think that could never happen in the UK, but when the government empowers Transport for London to bankrupt you because they believe you *might* have evaded your bus fare, quite frankly anything could happen. Such threats to liberty are exactly the sort of thing that Parliament *should* be discussing — rather than being nodded through with adjustments to rules on the size of eggs. Measures that affect legislation need to be prioritized, separated from the trivia, and debated in full.

Closer scrutiny of the *effects* of legislation is required. Over the last decade or more, the UK has moved closer to a presidential style of government. But the new president, in Downing Street, still controls the lawmaking arm of government, in Westminster. The result is that government has become seamlessly politicised, as I outlined in my book *The Rotten State of Britain*. Ministers promote bills not for the public good, but as a way of advertising and promoting themselves. The party apparatchiks in Downing Street decide what is good for us; the cabinet merely discusses spin; civil servants' advice is brushed aside; ministers present bills to Parliament without even having read them; government MPs do not bother reading them either, because everyone knows they have the majority. So quarter-baked laws are enacted and the headlines are captured. Gradually their contradictions and injustices become clear; but by then, the spin-doctors have moved on to other issues.

To counter this development we need a UK version of the Contract with America that was promoted by the US Republicans in 1994. They promised to make Congress subject to the same laws as everyone else; to get an independent accounting firm to audit waste, fraud and abuse; and to promote a balanced budget and twelve-year maximum terms on all elected representatives. We also need the equivalent of the 1989 US President's Council on Competitiveness, and subject every major legislative and regulatory proposal to analysis by economists and accountants to challenge the spin and calculate their real economic burden on businesses and individuals in terms of lost jobs, competitiveness, and trade.

Cutting the number of MPs

The large number of new MPs coming into Parliament in 2010 could be a powerful force for reform. They have no reason to fall in with the existing system, especially in view of how distrusted it is. If they got together — and they might need a couple of shop stewards pushing them — they could really reform Parliament, wrest its powers back from Downing Street, question ministers more effectively, assert their right to challenge Whitehall directly, and recover Parliament's position as the voice of the people, restraining government's centralisation and bullying.

But how many MPs do we need? The Conservatives, in September 2009, suggested a 10% cut in numbers, which seems pretty pathetic. Sir John Major in November 2009 said there should be a cut of more like 20%. We should go much further. The US House of Representatives has just 441 members for a population five times larger than the UK, yet American democracy remains very vigorous. Ambler and Boyfield also argue for drastic cuts — but with Assistant MPs (rather like Legislative Assistants in Congress) who can take up local issues, allowing MPs themselves to focus on the more important national debates.

In the days when an MP had to ride half a day to talk to a constituent, small constituencies made sense. Modern communications remove that need. We could surely lose a third of our parliamentarians without anyone (apart from them) shedding a tear. That would need extensive boundary changes — which must happen anyway, because constituencies vary hugely in size (from 22,000 voters in the Western Isles to 110,000 in the Isle of Wight), and the boundaries are about a decade behind population movements, which is why Labour in 2005 won 56% of the seats in Parliament with just 36% of the votes cast in the country. Quite why it takes a decade to sort out boundaries that an ordinary desktop computer could calculate in about ten minutes remains one of the deeper mysteries of parliamentary 'democracy'.

Curbing party self-interest
The power of the political parties in our democracy needs to be trimmed. At present, candidates for election to Parliament are chosen behind closed doors by local party executives — though often their party HQ tries to shoehorn favoured candidates into safe seats. The party headquarters also vet potential candidates, not allowing their name to go forward to the selection boards unless it approves them. A large majority of those chosen are political careerists who started in student politics, got themselves onto a school board and then their local council, and worked for a political party or a trade union, a think-tank, or some campaign group.

To break down this careerist party selection system and encourage more real candidates to come forward, Carswell and Hannan suggest a system of open primaries, like those in the United States, where candidates are chosen in open ballots of all voters who are prepared to register with their preferred party — or even by all voters.

Most US states enable you to register with a party when

you register to vote. In many states, the parties allow their registered voters to vote in a 'closed primary' to help select Congressional candidates. Others run 'open primaries' in which any voter can cast a vote for any party's candidate. (Louisiana is known for its 'jungle' primaries, in which anyone can stand, and anyone can vote.) In some states, a candidate needs 50% of the vote to win the nomination, so there is a series of runoffs to whittle down the candidates. There are other methods too: Virginia Republicans nominate their candidates at conventions — though this means electors having to travel to the state capital to participate.

Already, the Conservatives have experimented with the idea of primaries. They held one to choose their (successful) London mayoral candidate, Boris Johnson. In August 2009, a primary in which nearly a quarter of the electorate took part picked Dr Sarah Wollaston as Conservative parliamentary candidate for Totnes. And they announced an 'all postal' primary is Gosport to find a replacement for Sir Peter Viggers (of duck house fame).

The idea is plainly worth exploring. In the UK, primaries might be more easily and conducted by mail ballots rather than through the US tradition of public meetings. Parties could even hold virtual 'conventions' and allow people to vote online. All such ideas would encourage independent-minded candidates to come forward, reduce the power of the political party machines, and keep the political parties more in touch with the electorate — which must all be for the good.

The public should also be consulted on other matters. We need referendums on contentious laws — the 42-day detention without trial plan, for example — and on any further constitutional change, including EU treaties. Why do our politicians assume that they are the only people capable of making crucial decisions? Why do they not, occasionally, just ask the people?

Why the House of Lords should be different
The old hereditary peerage had a lot going for it. Random accidents of birth gave the House of Lords more women, more people with disability, more racial minorities, more young people, more old people, more communists, more people with no party affiliation, more non-lawyers and more non-careerists than the House of Commons ever had. But it had an inbuilt Conservative majority and no democratic legitimacy, so a new system was needed. Life peers changed the political balance slightly, and allowed more people of distinction to join the House. Yet far too many life peers were just superannuated hacks, 'kicked upstairs' to make way for younger candidates, or ennobled as compensation for losing elections. It all made the House of Lords the UK's biggest quango, its membership — like so much in politics — decided on the basis of the prime minister's patronage.

People have talked about House of Lords reform for decades, but nobody agrees on how to do it. For democratic legitimacy, it would have to be elected; but then it might become just another, politicised House of Commons, and lose its more detached, long-term view of things. Elections are unlikely to produce candidates with the expertise and independence of mind of some appointed peers, such as Lord Winston or the Chief Rabbi, who are valuable to our legislative process, but who may be unwilling to put themselves forward in an election.

The current proposal is therefore another piecemeal change, envisaging an 80% elected House of Lords, with the bishops staying in place, but the 92 hereditary peers going. There is an idea to move to a 100% elected chamber at some future time, but on past experience, that may never happen. Before we start rushing off to organise elections, though, we should first ask what it is that we want the House of Lords actually to do? Once we have decided that, we can decide how best to recruit the right members.

The Lords — or whatever it is rebranded — needs to be more than a look-alike Commons, packed full of the same party careerists. The virtue of the Lords has always been its expertise, experience, longer-term vision, greater distance from party politics, and focus on the basic legal rights of the individual. It was the House of Lords, for example, that killed Jacqui Smith's proposal for the police to be able to hold people without charge for 42 days. The House of Lords has a deeper feeling for our fundamental liberties than do our media-driven, populist MPs. It is not that its members are particularly liberal, it is just that they are less bothered about headlines.

To detach the new chamber from everyday politics we should make the term of office long — say seven years — and not allow people to stand for re-election. Party bosses would then have no leverage over them. (If they called themselves 'Lord' for ever more, just as American ex-presidents are still called 'Mr President', few of us would grudge them the courtesy title.) There remains the problem that elections attract naturally political, self-promoting political campaigners — when what we really want is a body of serious experts who can bring wisdom to the national debate. Maybe a limit of zero on election expenses could help, though it would favour existing celebrities rather than people who are able but little known. A ban on using party descriptions might encourage more serious people to stand, without having their reputations tainted by party labels.

Plainly, the election system must be *different*. The Lords cannot just be elected on the same basis as the Commons, or it will be a mere copy of that discredited house. Probably the worst idea is to have it elected by a party list system, like the European elections, which simply entrenches the power of the parties even more deeply. We want Parliament to represent our interest, not the interests of our political class.

In the United States, the House of Representatives is elected on a per capita basis, and the Senate on the basis of two people from each state: so that smaller states who lose out in one have more influence in the other. The Lords too could be constructed to reflect the diversity of the population that the Commons presently misses. The possibilities are endless. But what we need is a lengthy public debate, rather than rushing through change just because a half-reformed Lords is a nagging anomaly for politicians who like things tidy. The Lords should be the longstop of our liberty, our last defence against bullying governments: it is worth getting it right.

Devolving power from Westminster

We also need to think of our Westminster representation in the context of the devolved legislatures. Proud though Scotland is of its Parliament, and Wales and Northern Ireland are of their assemblies, they have not been the best solution. The cost of an extra tier of government, the tedium of an extra round of elections, and the poor calibre of those elected, are all common complaints. It would have been far easier and cheaper for the Westminster Parliament to sit for three days a week to discuss UK-wide issues, and for the Welsh and

Scottish MPs to form themselves into national parliaments, discussing devolved issues, for another two.

Devolution today suffers from the fact that it was a political, rather than a constitutional, initiative, rushed through by the Blair government solely to secure Labour's dominance of Scotland and Wales, and keep the Conservatives out of them for ever. Unfortunately the plan backfired: against the backdrop of greater national independence, Labour came to look more like colonial powers than national champions, and the rise of the nationalist parties have left them with lasting headaches.

Now people in England calling for a Parliament of their own. The idea has something to commend it, as my colleague Madsen Pirie outlined in the 2009 Adam Smith Institute book, *Zero Base Policy*. It could solve, for example, the West Lothian Problem — why an MP from West Lothian should be able to vote on schools and hospitals across England, but not on schools and hospitals in West Lothian. With a separate Parliament of English MPs deciding these matters for their own country, this problem fades away.

An English Parliament can be created without needing any new buildings — which is a relief: the Scottish Parliament building was estimated to cost £40 million but ended up costing over £400 million — and without any new round of elections. It would simply be formed by English MPs in Westminster.

Carswell and Hannan would go even further, and give the English counties the same sorts of powers that the Scottish Parliament has over schools, healthcare, local taxation and other subjects. Again, that would help plug the democratic deficit without needing any new buildings or extra tier of government at all.

Parliament's relationship with local authorities needs to be redefined. The Conservative *Control Shift* policy document sees a major devolution of powers from Parliament down to the local authorities and ultimately to individuals and families. It foresees elected mayors in the larger cities, and powers for local electors to veto council tax rises and to instigate local referendums.

Much of *Control Shift* is about removing the regional tier of government, such as the regional development agencies. (What do these bodies *do* anyway? They are unaccountable, have a huge secretariat and little expertise. We should scrap them and give the money back to the counties.) The strategic health authorities could go too. (Lord Kalms, who built the high street electronics chain Curry's into a national giant, told me that he always used to bin any memo with the word 'strategy' in the heading, as shifting management's attention away from customers. The NHS could learn much from this approach.) Then there are the government regional offices, learning and skills councils, and plenty more. Their roles are ill-defined, they are not properly accountable, and they make services more rather than less remote from the public.

Trust the locals — or better, the people
Though many people welcome the idea of less centralisation in government, they worry about the wisdom of devolving powers down to local authorities, since local councillors are generally pretty useless. Yet there are two answers to this.

Firstly, the imperative must be to devolve decisions down *beyond* local authorities, to people themselves, wherever we can. It is not about simply holding local elections for every public job, or electing boards to run schools, hospitals and social services departments.

On that score, my own record with 'local democracy' is very bad. I got onto the local school board — there was not even an election — and discovered that school governors have absolutely no power at all. Small decisions are made by the staff, and large ones by the council. Likewise, I thought it would be a public service to make myself a member of the local hospital. Now they send me a ballot paper every year with four candidates on it who I do not know from a bar of soap. I have long since given up voting.

The same might happen with the idea of elected local sheriffs or police chiefs. It could happen that celebrity self-publicists or demagogues fill these roles, as they have done in the case of elected mayors. We should keep party politics out of policing, but if there are no party labels, how are the public to know who the candidates are — unless they are indeed self-publicists? Maybe the policy is worth a try: local people must feel in control of their own policing. But we should quickly abandon the idea if it has perverse effects.

Generally, though, we do not need politicians to run our lives. As we will see, for example, there is no reason why schools should be run by County Hall. Handing the budget directly to schools, who can then buy in shared services between themselves, cuts out a huge tier of officialdom; and making the state's money follow parents' choices through a schools voucher will steer taxpayers' money, without any need for bureaucracy, to the schools where parents actually want to see it spent.

Shifting the balance of taxation

The second answer is that we have to remember that local authorities presently raise only a quarter of their budget locally. The rest comes from Whitehall, and nearly all of that comes with a cat's cradle of strings attached. Councils have almost no say in how they raise and spend money, so it is not surprising that many able people cannot be bothered to serve on them. Radically shifting tax-raising powers out from the centre, would make it worth people getting involved in local government again. There would be real local debate on priorities and costs, and good people would step forward for election.

There would have to be some new form of local taxation. Today's council tax, which is largely a tax on buildings, is not up to the job. Most people have only one home, from which they do not want to move, and although their home keeps them warm and dry, it does not produce an income. So people on low incomes, like pensioners, would find it very hard to pay more — indeed, there are complaints even at its present levels.

In the 2004 Adam Smith Institute report *Paying For Localism*, Douglas Carswell proposed a local sales tax, replacing VAT, similar to the system in America. But the UK is a small country, and some local authorities have little in the way of shopping centres, and would lose out from this. To replace VAT would get us into protracted arguments with the European Union; while keeping it and adding a sales tax would make life impossible for traders.

I have therefore concluded that the best way to finance an enhanced local democracy would be a local income tax — much like the municipal income tax that other European countries use. It would be easy and cheap to collect, being just another line on the income tax form: Whitehall would collect the money and farm it out to the local authorities. And it would also make it easy to demonstrate that national taxes were being cut in line with the rise in local taxes — and that the new local tax was not simply adding to people's burden.

Yet there are problems, as there are with all local taxes. The tax may be set locally, but it is collected by and distributed from the centre, which still leaves a lot of clout in Whitehall. Furthermore, there are some localities where incomes are extremely low, so inevitably there has to be some mechanism to transfer money from rich to poor areas (though this may be better done through the benefits system). Such a mechanism once again puts a great deal of financial control into central hands: national politicians would have to be very strong to resist the temptation to attach strings to the hand-outs. But why not go down the route of Denmark, and instead have the equalisation payments decided by the local authorities themselves, mediating it through the Local Government Association?

Public limits on council power
If councils have the power to raise local taxes, what is to stop taxing and spending wildly? In the United States, local government budgets cannot take effect until they are approved by the electorate, which is done at the local elections. So there is an open debate about spending: the budget is published in the press, talked about at town meetings and on local TV and radio. The result is a much better informed electorate, fully aware of the role and activities of their local representatives, and a wider under-standing of how local taxes, costs and services are connected. If voters reject the budget, the authorities have to go back to the drawing board and propose a new one. It seems a good model for the UK.

Indeed, much more can be done through local referendums, held at the same time as council elections. It is remarkable how many decisions that are decided centrally in the UK are made locally in other countries. In the United States, for example, bans on smoking in public places have been enacted purely locally. That allows a variety of different approaches to be compared, instead of the UK-style, one-size-fits-all central smoking policy that has led to the death of so many of our pubs and clubs. Issues like supermarket planning applications should also be decided by local referendum. It would spark a real local debate, and get people engaged; and it would force the supermarkets to be more aware of the concerns of people who are affected, and to compensate them directly.

The courage to let go
Restoring our democracy will not be an easy job. It will require rebuilding the public's trust in Parliament. It will require self-restraint from the national politicians at the centre of power. It will require constitutional changes to reassert the role of Parliament as the representative of the people against an over-mighty central government. It will require tax changes to push control out from the centre and back to the localities and to individuals. But centralised power corrupts and spreads, as we have seen over recent decades. To restore our liberties and put power back into the hands of the individuals and families from which it ultimately derives, will be a huge challenge; but there is no prize greater for any enlightened government, nor effort more worthwhile.

5

BUREAUCRACY

CUTS ARE NECESSARY

Andrew Haldenby is head of the think-tank Reform. He is lean and looks slightly nervous, as if he needs to keep moving in order to dodge the fusillade of ideas that are constantly spraying around his Westminster offices. Reform has a way with words — it was one of their reports, by Nick Bosanquet and Blair Gibbs, that coined the phrase 'the IPOD generation' — the Insecure, Pressurised, Over-taxed, Debt-ridden young of today. And Andrew himself has a nice turn of phrase to describe what has happened to our public services.

'A flash flood of taxpayers' money has swept through the public sector,' he says. And like every flash flood, this one has overwhelmed the natural channels of public spending and brought destruction in its wake. Public services like health and education were simply unable to cope with the new money welling over them. Not surprisingly, a large amount of it was sluiced into higher wages and salaries for government workers, rather than driving the millwheels of public service delivery.

Time for action on civil service productivity
Indeed, in a decade (1997–2007) when productivity in the

private sector grew by more than a quarter (27.9%), public-sector productivity actually *declined* by 3.4%, according to the Centre for Economic and Business Research (CEBR). The UK now ranks 76th out of 134 countries in terms of public service efficiency, more than halfway down the table. Looking at the amount of public spending that goes on wages, roughly £250 billion a year, CEBR calculate that if public sector costs and productivity had matched those in the private sector, taxpayers would be £60 billion better off. For that amount of money, we could have scrapped VAT or cut income tax bills by more than two-fifths.

One reason for the public sector's poor productivity is that government workers throw more sickies than the rest of us — an average of nearly ten days sick leave (costing £784) per employee each year. That is roughly a third (3.3 days) more than the average in the private sector. Public bodies pay sick pay longer, and they are less likely to discipline staff for unacceptable absence or restrict their sick pay. It is a seriously large waste of money.

Also, while the private sector has been shedding jobs, employment in central and local government, public corporations and the civil service has continued to rise — to around 5.75 million public employees (or 6 million if you include the state-run banks). Likewise, in 2009 when private firms have had to freeze cut wages, public employees such as council workers, police, NHS staff and even MPs still received inflation-matching increases.

Curbing Town Hall and Whitehall top salaries
Not that some public employees are underpaid. The TaxPayers Alliance calculated that in 2007/08 there were over 1,000 people in the country's town halls on salaries over

£100,000, some 193 earning more than cabinet ministers, sixteen earning more than the prime minister and nine earning over £200,000. It was not easy for the TPA to come by this information, since — unlike private companies — local authorities do not have to show how much their executives are paid.

In government departments, quangos, public corporations, nationalised industries and other public bodies, 806 people got payment packages worth £150,000 or more in 2008/09. Nearly five hundred of them earned more than the prime minister, even the head of Whitehall's wheelie bin quango. Thirty-five of them earn more than £500,000 and there were even eight who pulled in more than £1 million, including the heads of Network Rail, the Royal Mail and Channel 4. Perhaps most remarkable, in the previous year there were ten people working in the Treasury, the Bank of England and the FSA — in other words, the people who oversaw the financial crisis — who earned on average more than £400,000, and 24 executives who presided over embarrassing losses of personal data received packages worth £190,000.

But it is not just Whitehall and Town Hall fatcats who do well from the taxpayer. Public employees in general earn more on average than do people in the private sector. Indeed, the average pay gap between them has been increasing, from a 1.1% gap in 1985 to a 3.3% gap in 2005.

Scrap gold-plated public sector pensions
Public sector workers get perks that are simply unaffordable in the private sector. Around 20 million workers in the private sector have no final salary pension, though they pay taxes so that state employees can enjoy these generous schemes — under which they retire at 60 (compared to the private sector

norm of 65), on pensions equal to two-thirds of their salary, fully indexed against inflation (compared to the private sector norm of a 2.5% inflation cap — if any).

Civil servants live longer than the rest of us, so they get paid benefits for longer, yet there are also generous provisions for early retirement on health grounds. About 70% of firefighters, 50% of police officers, and 25% of doctors and teachers make use of this, while only 20% of private sector workers retire early on health grounds. The whole thing is a scam: civil servants who retire on full pension at 50 get jobs elsewhere, or are even hired back as 'consultants' to do the same job, while police officers under investigation for wrongdoing find it convenient to quit the force early, pocket their pension, and escape further questioning.

Meanwhile a fifth of the council tax we pay goes to retired, rather than active, council workers. Some police forces pay out more in pensions to retired officers than they do in wages. A senior civil servant (or a second-ranker in London) on a salary of £54,000 is entitled to a pension of two-thirds of that, or £36,000 a year. If you or I wanted to retire on £36,000 a year, we would need about £1 million in the bank to fund it. To assemble that amount of money, I figure that we would have to save £13,800 a year at 3% interest over our forty-year working lives. That amounts to just over a quarter of the civil servant's £54,000 salary after tax, and more if we take tax into account.

The bottom line is that the UK's civil servants, public sector workers, and even MPs all receive a hidden pension pay boost that mounts up to between just under a third (29%) and just over two-fifths (42%) of their stated salaries.

Ending the public sector pension bonanza

Not surprisingly, public sector unions have been so desperate to protect this concealed subsidy from taxpayers that they have expansively agreed to contribute a little more themselves. Health workers, whose pension plan has liabilities of £165 billion or more, now pay at least 5% of their salaries towards their pension, with those earning more than £100,000 paying 8.5%. Also, new recruits to most public sector pension schemes will now have to wait until 65 to retire, instead of getting their pension at 60.

Fiddling about by making new recruits retire at 65 and pay a bit more into their own pension pot is not going to solve the cost problem — nor the fairness problem, in that public employees both earn more, and get more generous pensions, than private employees. We must take a hard line on public sector pensions. We cannot tear up existing pension entitlements. But we should stop future gold-plated pension commitments stone dead and start afresh.

As Nigel Hawkins said in his 2009 Adam Smith Institute report *Ten Economic Priorities*, the fairest and most economical option would be to close all public sector final-salary schemes to new recruits entirely, and move those workers to what is now the norm in the private sector — at least, the norm where people have any pension at all — namely 'defined benefit' plans, where the worker and employer both contribute into a pension pot which on retirement pays out whatever the size of the pot allows, regardless of past salary.

Cutting the size of the Cabinet

The Conservatives have pledged to cut Whitehall by a third — though much of that may come from just eliminating a few managers and shipping civil servants out of London, rather than from serious cuts in the bureaucracy. But do we really need all this government at all? The state sector has grown by half since 1997: does anyone really imagine all that is necessary?

A defining moment came in June 2009 when Gordon Brown proudly showed off his new, reshuffled cabinet before the television cameras. I thought it odd that they were sitting in one of Downing Street's upstairs reception rooms, around trestle tables of the sort you see in church halls. What happened to the boat-shaped table, with its William IV tripod legs, introduced by Harold Macmillan so that the prime minister could see everyone? The answer was that Brown's cabinet had grown too big for the cabinet table. And with all of the additional minister, czars, advisers and officials who now attend cabinet meetings, the squash had become impossible.

You cannot make decisions with a cabinet of this size. People who sit on boards know that the smaller they are, the better, and that the maximum practical size is about eleven. (Jesus had twelve disciples, say management gurus, and that proved to be one too many.) A plan to cut the cabinet to that size would concentrate our leaders' minds on just which departments of state were truly necessary and which were not.

We need:

* A prime minister, as a chief executive and communications director.
* A finance secretary, who looks after taxation and spending.
* A public service secretary, in charge of personnel

and reform.
* A defence secretary, in charge of the armed forces.
* A justice secretary, handling crime prevention, police, courts and prisons.
* A foreign secretary, handling foreign relations and foreign aid.
* An interior secretary, looking after issues of national identity and life, such as families, culture, immigration, major events, and the environment.
* A health secretary, promoting access to healthcare, public and private.
* An education secretary, shaping policy on schools and colleges.
* A welfare secretary, covering social security and pensions.
* A local affairs secretary, handling government's relationship with the localities.

That makes a conveniently sized cabinet of just eleven ministers. Out would go the business department, for a start. Madsen Pirie — President of the Adam Smith Institute (ASI), former secretary of the high-IQ society MENSA, and author of books on philosophy and logic — points out in his 2009 ASI report *Zero Base Policy* that, while is useful to have someone batting for business, it does not need an entire department of state. A minister at the Treasury could deal with UK business concerns, and one at the Foreign Office could help exporters. Otherwise, a business department makes work for idle hands, and business would be better off without its constant interference.

Out too would go the environment department (an important subject, but one that properly belongs in the interior ministry), energy (which goes along with environment), the cabinet office (the minister for public sector renewal handles all that), the chief secretary to the Treasury (a non-cabinet role within finance) and culture (which goes to the interior ministry). Scottish, Welsh, Northern Irish (and indeed English) issues are looked after by the local affairs crew. The cabinet will want to maintain communications with Parliament, so the leaders of both houses might sit in on meetings as observers, as might the government's law officer. Otherwise, what ministers do we really need?

Zero-base recruiting

What ministries do we really need, either? The culling of ministers in order to create a manageable cabinet needs to be reflected by a culling of ministries in order to create a manageable government.

Of course, this will never happen if it is left to civil servants. One reason why civil service numbers are so hard to keep down is because every time a prime minister reshuffles ministers and changes departmental responsibilities, Whitehall responds by simply adding new people alongside the existing workforce, rather than rationalising. By contrast, private sector mergers and acquisitions experts have thousandfold experience in managing changes of direction and purpose within companies, and in merging and rationalising different departments. When two major firms merge, for example, different production units are thrust together and back office duplication has to be eliminated. Customer contracts and supply systems are kept in place, so that frontline service delivery is not interrupted; but the contracts of all the managers are terminated, and they are invited to apply afresh for the new management positions that now exist within the changed structure, so that the best candidates can be selected. Government should be no different.

Why do 80,000 civil servants have to be located in and around Whitehall, one of the most expensive locations in London? Plainly, ministers need their key advisers close at hand, near Parliament (not that too many ministers bother showing up *there* these days). But most of the work can be distributed out to the regions, where property prices and salaries are lower. That would provide an opportunity to re-think exactly what personnel levels are required; and it might help people outside London to feel that their government is less remote, too.

Another way to cut costs and rationalise the workforce is zero base recruiting. Instead of jobs being routinely advertised and refilled as soon as anyone leaves, officials should have to make a convincing case that the particular job is strictly necessary. The London Borough of Hammersmith & Fulham has shown that large savings are possible though this approach, without any loss of service to the public. A freeze on automatic recruitment throughout the whole civil service could save £5 billion a year, even if front line posts like teachers, nurses and doctors were excluded. Right now, such savings are essential.

Curbing the quangos

Few people know how many non-departmental public bodies — quangos — there are these days, because the government simply conceals the information. One who does, though, is the country's leading quango hunter Dan Lewis, the russet-haired Chief Executive of the Economic Policy Centre, who has compiled several quango surveys for the Centre for Policy Studies. 'The government used to publish a 400-page list of quangos,' he says. 'But their growth began to get embarrassing — Blair created about 70 new ones — so after 2006 they simply omitted about 90% of them, hoping nobody would notice.'

That has left us with an official list of just 40 pages, which does not even include publicly financed by notionally independent bodies like Channel 4 and the BBC, or the Scottish, Welsh and Northern Irish quangos. So in the interests of transparency, the Economic Policy Centre is conducting its own full audit of quangos and their staff and salary costs. The quangocracy, it turns out, is a £90 billion business.

Lewis has less problem with the legions of advisory councils — doctors, teachers and other experts who advise ministers on policy issues for little more than the cost of a train fare to London and a sandwich lunch. What really gets his goat is the executive bodies like the Financial Services Authority. They are supposed to deliver a public service, but they never have to face a tender competition for that role. Unelected and accountable to nobody, they set their own rules — and can even fine or prosecute people who break them.

Most could simply be abolished, with no loss to the nation. There are lots of quangos in health and education in particular, all stepping on each other's feet and burying teachers and doctors in a snowstorm of circulars, guidance, policy and rules. The Blair government, anxious to show that it was getting a grip on schools and the NHS, set up several new ones after it was elected — only to abolish or merge them again within just a few years, at huge cost to the taxpaying public.

Lewis would scrap most of the agriculture quangos too. 'They are a legacy from the past, when agriculture was hugely more important to the UK economy than it is today,' he insists. He has a point: do we really need the Potato Council up in Kenilworth, trying to induce us to eat more potatoes with its 'lovechips' website and campaign? After all, it seems to fly in the face of all the food advice that various *health* quangos are aiming at us.

'The Carbon Trust and several other energy and environment quangos should all go too,' continues Lewis, who happens to be an energy and environment expert who has written extensively on the subject for the Economic Research Council, and knows what he is talking about. 'Theirs is a complete scattergun approach to the policy of trying to get us to use less fossil-based energy.' And I do wonder if all their full-page newspaper ads do any good at all.

Corin Taylor agrees on the need to cull a few quangos. Another thinker who is capable of firing out facts, figures, policies and ideas at machine-gun speed, he is now a senior policy adviser at the Institute of Directors, the national association of company bosses. Talking to him in the busy 'airport lounge' of the Institute's London HQ, surrounded by perhaps a hundred or more executives all checking their spreadsheets, doing deals on their mobile phones, and topping up their caffeine levels, he stiffens when I mention the bodies that the government has set up to deliver 'business support'.

'The government does have a role in promoting foreign investment in the UK, but we really need one body centred around the needs of business, not a vast number of them all doing their own thing,' he says. 'A lot of our members do not make use of bodies such as Business Link, and find the overall structure confusing when they do. It would be relatively simple to save taxpayers money by cutting down on overlapping functions, which would deliver a better service at the same time.'

The sunset of quangocracy

However, some quango-watchers would go further still. 'I can't imagine that the country would grind to a halt if we abolished the lot of them and had a long rethink about what we really needed,' says Tim Ambler, the avuncular former businessman and fellow at the London Business School, who writes on regulation for the British Chambers of Commerce and the Adam Smith Institute. 'Do we really need the grandly named Equalities and Human Rights Commission (EHRC)? The laws on racial and sexual discrimination have been there for decades, as everyone is fully aware. Do we really need a quango making a career out of reminding us, and trying to push the law into new areas? Shouldn't racial threats be a matter for the police to sort out, rather than some quango having to tell us how to behave?' He has a point: even the deputy Labour leader Harriet Harman blocked the £185,000 salary proposed for the quango's new chief executive in November 2009, saying the job was not worth that amount of money. And when we already have a Government Equalities Office, do we need the EHRC at all?

So what are we to do about the quangos? As far as the regulatory bodies are concerned, Ambler suggests sunset laws of the sort that operate in the United States and other countries — something which Tony Blair promised, but did not deliver, except in a couple of cases. Under these rules, public bodies would be given a limited lifespan — say five years — before they had to replace themselves by proper competition, with an independently chaired self-regulation. After that they would have to justify their existence all over again. It would prompt a public debate over whether they were really needed. Maybe this is a job for a reformed House of Lords.

Meanwhile, Ambler, a former joint managing director of a global business group, favours the technique used to whittle down management numbers when firms merge. He would keep the laws in place, but suspend all the quangos until we had worked out which ones we really need to keep, what they should do, and how big a staff they require to do the job. The quangocrats would have to reapply for their job and show us the costs and benefits of what they do for society.

This quango holiday would itself do much to reveal which ones we would, and would not, miss. Those that are reinstated would face annual performance targets and sunset clauses as already described.

Again, we can hardly expect the good and the great to come up with a radical redesign of the quango sector. The new minister for public service renewal should be in charge, and maybe a panel of businesspeople would have a much clearer take on the costs and benefits of the quangocracy.

We will need to keep some quangos. Things like the utilities regulators will still need to regulate utilities, at least until competition and self-regulation can be brought in. But they should focus on the *economic* regulation of their industries. The Blair/Brown government used them to load the utilities with all kinds of social costs and political objectives. Economic matters, such as price setting and tariffs, should be the regulators' purpose. Lastly, such quangos as are left should report to Parliament, making their accountability to the public transparent. If the House of Commons thinks itself too busy, the quangocrats could make their reports to a reformed House of Lords.

Cutting paperwork
Each year the state requires us to fill out more than a billion forms. The annual torrent of red tape also includes around 75,000 pages of new rules (and 25,000 pages of explanation). Nobody can possibly keep up with it.

When I visit the United States and have to fill out immigration forms, I am always amused by the routine paragraph headed 'Paperwork Reduction Act', in which the red tape brigade have to explain why the particular form is necessary. It often used to take half a page itself, which is hardly paperwork *reduction*; but I can see the point.

At the very least, official forms should state how long it might take people to fill them out — including thinking about it and getting together all the material they need. It might make civil servants conscious that their forms do have a cost to businesses and the public. Right now, there is no downside for them: they can ask for more and more information with complete impunity, knowing that you or I will face a fine or imprisonment if we do not provide it. Now if bureaucrats faced fines or jail for asking unnecessary questions — *that* would be a step in the right direction!

Small businesses should be exempted from most regulation and paperwork entirely. Staff in small businesses know that they are risky ventures and hardly expect the same protections as salaried employees of large corporations, or indeed departments of state. And complying with onerous regulations is a much larger imposition on small companies than large ones. There is no need to pass special laws about this: one Act of Parliament could exempt small businesses from large swathes of red tape, or indeed, the wide powers already granted to ministers might be sufficient for them to introduce small firm exemptions.

Involving the NAO

Sir Barnett Cocks, Clark of the House of Commons from 1962 to 1974, famously observed that 'A committee is a cul-de-sac down which ideas are lured and then quietly strangled.' He also noted that the Houses of Parliament, which were completed about 150 years ago, were three times over budget (£2.4 million, against an estimate of £800,000), and 24 years behind schedule.

This is nothing unusual in government projects. For the cost of the NHS computer system, for example, it would be possible to buy every one of the 1.4 million people employed there a web enabled laptop — plus another ten for each of them to forget and leave on the train. IT projects do seem to be the worst, since civil servants have a mania for buying completely new bespoke systems, which end up getting more and more complicated, rather than buying software off the shelf and tweaking it as necessary. Private businesses can manage these things — one never hears of hotel or airline booking systems coming in years late, being full of bugs, and costing billions — so why can we not learn from them? Every time Whitehall contemplates some new computer gizmo, they should talk to private sector *users* of large software systems, and not just the *producers* who want to sell them kit. Indeed, private sector users should be hired to manage the whole process.

When Margaret Thatcher was swinging her handbag and

privatising a string of state industries, the Treasury built up a body of how-to-do-it expertise that could apply its experience to one enterprise after another. Techniques that worked well could be re-used the next time, and unsuccessful approaches shelved, without everyone having to re-learn everything afresh each time. Dan Lewis suggests that exactly the same idea should apply to the procurement and management of large government projects such as IT systems, the Olympics and infrastructure. The National Audit Office (NAO), he thinks, should be involved in big projects right at the start — currently they are only called in once things have become totally messed up, which is pretty much every time — so they can help civil servants to avoid mistakes in how the project is put together. It seems like a very sensible idea.

Being forensic auditors, the NAO might also be less sympathetic to the crony businesses that hang around government IT and construction projects, and who always seem to be invited to bid on new projects, even if they messed up a string of old ones. Perhaps civil servants believe their IT projects have to be *national* and therefore very big, meaning that only a few firms have the scale needed to manage them. Private firms, by contrast, are much more sanguine about letting local offices choose their own small-scale systems — provided that they can all talk to each other. Sure, you don't get the Order of the Bath for being involved in small-scale projects. But you might save taxpayers a lot of money, and stem the appalling corruption of business that occurs today.

Lewis thinks there are also lots of small things that the public sector can do to keep down its costs and generate revenue that helps limit all our tax bills. Look at all the thousands and thousands of government web pages, for example (which probably run into the millions if you include the BBC's). Why should they not carry Google ads, as commercial websites do? Why does the government not use print-on-demand agencies like Lulu or Lightningsource, instead of having vast warehouses full of official reports? Why are rail stations and the ground floors of government buildings not developed into commercial centres?

Online spending transparency

While we are at it, we should make it much easier for the private sector to compete for work that is presently done by public sector bodies. Why does the BBC get £3 billion from taxpayers (which, incidentally, allows it to pay 46 of its executives more than the prime minister)? It gets that money because it provides 'public service' broadcasting, we are told. Yes, and it provides a lot of other junk too, and runs a huge website that crowds out other potential content providers, a form of taxpayer subsidised competition against private companies. Why don't we simply put the public service broadcasting element — the £200 million or whatever that is spent so that politicians can preen themselves on *Newsnight* or the *Today Programme* — out to tender, and let Sky or ITV or anyone else bid to do those bits, and save ourselves a cool £2.8 billion? (The answer is probably because the BBC Trust, which runs things, has a split personality. It is supposed to represent the public interest, but then it also represents the Corporation itself. It cannot be both poacher and gamekeeper.) The BBC should run itself like any business, and some other independent panel or trust or even committee of Parliament should decide whether the public is getting good value. Or not.

The Royal Mail, to take another example of unfair competition, does not pay VAT on its business contracts, as private mail carriers do. Its vans are even able to stop on double yellow lines without getting a ticket, which again does not apply to private carriers. It is hardly a level playing field for competition. If, after our culling of the quangos, the Office of Fair Trading (OFT) still survives, this seems exactly the sort of anti-competitive wheeze it should kill stone dead.

There needs to be a great deal more transparency in how the public sector operates, particularly in how it spends money. The United States has made a start with its USAspending.gov site, but Grover Norquist of Americans for Tax Reform (ATR) wants to see every cheque that government bodies write posted on the web (with limited national security exemptions), so that all taxpayers could see how their money has been spent. He would also put all government contracts online, so we could see what our local and national politicians were signing up to.

Of course, that would generate far more information than most of us could handle: but specialist groups like ATR would gladly trawl through and highlight questionable spending. At both local and national level, it would spark real debate. Local businesses would soon point out how they could have provided the same goods or services for less money — increasing the competition among government suppliers. And the newspapers would delight in exposing overspending, backhanders and nepotism, just as the *Daily Telegraph* did with MPs' expenses. It is such a good idea, in fact, that Barack Obama, when still a US Senator from Illinois, was one of the signatories to the initial legislative proposals on the idea.

Indeed, online spending transparency 'could be as revolutionary in terms of how government works as the Freedom of Information Act has been,' says Matthew Elliott, the tireless head of the Taxpayers Alliance, whose views on public spending are quoted daily in some newspaper or other. All that is needed to make such spending transparency work, he believes, is an 'open architecture', like the COINS software used by leading private construction companies, which allows information to be pulled off the web and processed by anyone else. It does not need yet another ten-year public IT project, he insists. Already, Windsor & Maidenhead council publishes all payments over £500 each quarter, and Mid Sussex publishes them monthly. The Greater London Authority (GLA) publishes all expenditure over £1,000. The systems and the expertise are already there. We need to make all public expenditure transparent, and *quickly*, before even more billions are wasted.

Waste and abuse of public money would be revealed by the simple measure of posting government purchases online. Take the £38 million that public bodies spend — on consultants, trade associations, policy campaigns and think tanks — promoting themselves and trying to influence politicians to increase their powers and budgets even further. Consider, at this time of national restraint, the £45 million to give the British Film Institute new offices with five digital cinemas, or the £50 million extension to the Tate Modern, or even the £10 million for a new visitor centre at Stonehenge. Plus all the various groups that get government grants of one sort or another, like the £113,000 paid through Haringey Council (who brought us Victoria Climbié and Baby P) to fund three schools run by members of the extremist Islamic group Hizb ut-Tahrir, which Tony Blair once described as 'fanatical' and promised to ban. Putting such stuff promptly on the web would allow the public to raise its concerns, which is a lot better than finding out about them two years later, when the accounts are published.

Exposing and selling state assets

Another useful control would be an up to date, online Domesday Book of central and local government assets. When I met Corin Taylor at the Institute of Directors, I noted all the huge portraits of nineteenth-century military officers which graced every wall. 'Yes,' he said. 'This used to be the United Service Club, and we have to look after the pictures. It was built on the site of George IV's Carlton House, and it is still owned by the Crown Estate.' The Institute of Directors — still owned by the Crown Estate? *Why*, I wonder? And as I look more deeply into this grand body, I find it owns various imposing properties in central London, huge areas of forest, farmland and foreshore, Ascot racecourse, various famous Scottish estates including Glenlivet, and much more besides. Now tell me: should civil servants really be using taxpayers' money to play in the property management business?

Or running commercial businesses, for that matter? In his 2008 Adam Smith Institute paper *Privatisation: Reviving the Momentum*, City analyst Nigel Hawkins identified £20 billion worth of enterprises that the government simply did not really need to own. They included ports, water utilities, railway companies, Channel 4, the London tube, the Royal Mail and even a bookmaker, the Tote.

A year later, Gordon Brown agreed to sell many of these assets — though by then it was a fire sale and their value had halved. It is plainly not worth selling these assets now, when nobody (except maybe the governments of China and various

Middle Eastern countries) can afford to buy them. Instead, these businesses should be put on a workout so that they are in shape to be sold when world markets recover. On sticking points like the huge pension liabilities of Royal Mail, the taxpayer just has to take the hit: businesses with liabilities like that just cannot be shifted. But even that is better than the public being held to ransom by state monopolies.

Holding the bureaucracy to account

Having wasted days or weeks trying to find accurate statistics on the public sector, I am painfully aware that the online information from the Office for National Statistics (ONS) is a mess. Stuff is hidden in a forest of tables; basic information is hidden away and, when you find it, is not presented in simple or logical formats. Why *should* it take hours to find simple numbers like the number of people employed in the public sector, and what they are paid? Apart from the core numbers — the national accounts, employment, population, and price data — most of what is online is useful only to specialists, who frankly ought to pay for their esoteric information. Otherwise, the rest of us get pretty poor value for the £200 million we pay for the ONS each year.

Is this perhaps another agency whose work should be contracted out to private sector providers? It should certainly be more independent of government. As should the Information Commissioner (who reports, not to Parliament, but to the Justice department), and the National Audit Office (which has to agree its reports with individual departments). All these bodies should properly be accountable to our representatives in Parliament, not to the government, which tries to distort their findings for its own political convenience.

As a simple courtesy to the voter, the National Audit

Office should send every household a yearly receipt for all the cash they generously pay out to support their government. Your income: £30,400. Taxes you pay directly: £7,400. Indirect taxes you pay: £4,900. Your share of government borrowing: well, it is rising so fast that the numbers would just be a blur. Bottom line: well over half your income spent. And what have you bought with it? NHS healthcare (whether you use it or not): £2,300. Schools (ditto): £1,700. State pensions for other people: £2,300. Welfare benefits: £2,100. Transport ... well, you get the picture.

It might bring home to people just how much they are paying for very little benefit. It might even get the public involved in that central question which my proposed minister for public service renewal has to answer — how can the whole machinery of government be reformed to provide just the essentials, better and cheaper?

People power over the purse
Ultimately, though, as my Georgian friend Lado Gurgenidze points out, the only way to curb the relentless growth of government and its agencies is to starve it of the oxygen of public money — money that is taken from us under threat of imprisonment, making it quite an easy steal. Lado points to the state of Colorado, which changed its constitution in 1994, bringing in a Taxpayer Bill of Rights (TaBoR); and campaigners in other states from Maine to California would like to do something similar.

The idea of TaBoR is to set overall limits to government's total tax take. Large tax increases have to be approved by referendum. It takes the power of the purse back from legislators and puts it firmly into the hands of the people. Which, after all, is where it should belong.

6

EDUCATION

In the great flash flood of public spending that has occurred since the end of the 1990s, those working in our health and education sectors have made out like bandits (GPs and school heads can now easily earn over £100,000). Budgets have soared, and the largest part of the extra cash has gone into wages. Yet outputs have not soared to match, and indeed productivity has fallen. To a general public who have had to tighten their own belts during the recession, it seems unfair. They want to see reform, and they want it now.

Improving exams
It is astonishing how we can educate young people for eleven years (Gordon Brown's plan was to make it thirteen) and yet still turn tens of thousands of them out into the street either functionally illiterate or with no meaningful qualification at all. Yes, having 98% of students pass their exams is impressive, and more kids are getting the targeted 5 A*-C grades at GCSE, but do those grades mean much any more? In Edexcel's maths exam for 2008, a score of 36 out of 100 got you a C — which is officially a 'good' grade, while 9 out of 100 got you an E — a pass. Get roughly one in three

answers right, in other words, and you are 'good'. Get less than one in ten right and you still pass.

With mock exams, end of year exams, SATs and GCSEs themselves, parents and educationalists both complain that there is no time for kids to explore subjects beyond what is going to be in the exam. But in the world of state education, driven entirely from the centre in Whitehall, it is the exam that counts. Schools and teachers are rewarded for getting good exam results; exam boards are keen to help them. So the boards give elaborate guidance on how to get students through the exam, and teachers drill and coach their kids so that they pass. They give them 'writing frames' and specimen answers to copy; they suggest revisions to their coursework and do not submit it until they think it might pass muster; they focus on turning D grades into the target C grades, rather than stretching the brighter students; they refuse to submit borderline kids for the examination, so as to keep their pass rates looking good; they steer pupils into subjects that are easy passes, not necessarily what the kids themselves need.

Employers and universities no longer trust school examinations. Employers talk of annual 'grade inflation' and the top universities such as Cambridge already have five times more candidates with three or more A* and A grades than they can accept, so rely on their own entrance examinations and interviews instead. It would, perhaps, make much more sense to cut out the bureaucracy and have the examination system designed and run by the universities and employers, rather than a quango in London.

And quangos there are aplenty. They have been created, reformed, merged, and reformed again all in the space of a decade. Do we really need a Qualifications and Curriculum Development Agency (QCDA) or an Ofqual, which both emerged from the Qualifications and Curriculum Authority (QCA)? As the educationalist Tom Burkard says in his 2009 Centre for Policy Studies paper, *School Quangos*, a small advisory board drawn from the universities and employers would quickly tell you what the curriculum should cover and whether exam standards were slipping. Burkard would get rid of plenty more characters in the alphabet soup, such as the TDA, the NCSL, STRB, PFS and BECTA (don't ask what they all mean, it would take too long) — with a potential saving of £633 million. After all, independent schools seem to achieve better results without being bossed around by all these quangocrats. (Mimicking the wartime travel poster, governments should ask themselves: Is Your Quango Really Necessary?)

Initiatives rather than reform

Despite plenty of Whitehall name changes — the old Department of Education and Science became the Department for Education and Employment, then the Department for Education and Skills, then the Department for Children, Schools and Families — politicians have found the state school system almost impossible to reform. So instead they have resorted to inventing all sorts of new kinds of school that they hope will be better. Mrs Thatcher brought in Specialist Schools and City Technology Colleges, which became City Academies, and then just Academies under Blair. In another giant leap for the 'diversity agenda', universities and businesses were encouraged to create yet another variety of school, the Trust Schools. And so it goes on.

The trouble is that the system is not diverse at all. Whitehall sets down increasingly detailed rules on what schools teach, how they teach it, where they teach it, and to whom they teach it. There is little opportunity for schools to be different, nor for parents to choose between them. 'We enjoy running the diversity agenda,' one Whitehall mandarin told me, as if diversity and central control were entirely compatible.

Politicians too try to dictate how schools are run, with almost constant directives and initiatives. It was brought home to me a few years back, when I became a school governor. One day, the local authority representative on the board came in and announced that the minister had earmarked money to fund better disabled access arrangements in schools, and that we should bid for some. After about twenty minutes speculating about where we might put in ramps and suchlike, I asked the politically incorrect question of how many disabled students we had. Of course, we had none. 'This is ridiculous,' I said. 'What we really need money for is things like renovating the boys' toilets, which are absolutely disgusting.' Suddenly eyes lit up. 'That's perfect,' said another governor. 'If we make them *disabled* toilets, we will get the money.'

Even the Conservatives think they know best. In 2009 they expansively promised to build a new Technical School in each of the twelve biggest cities in England, complete with Academy status. How do they know that the twelve biggest cities in England actually *want* new Technical Schools? Perhaps parents should decide, rather than politicians.

Introducing competition

What the system cannot stand is competition. Robert Whelan — Cambridge graduate, Deputy Director of the think-tank Civitas, and author of books on the history of voluntary action — also runs the New Model School Company. He and colleagues like the Civitas Director Dr David Green set it up in order to deliver affordable non-state education for children aged 4–11. The company keeps costs down by finding space in community centres and church halls rather than having its own, expensive school buildings. As the schools (and there are three of them) grow, the idea is to move them into full-size premises.

Naturally, the schools regulator Ofsted and the department in Whitehall are a complete thorn in the side of this initiative. Although independent schools are not obliged to teach the national curriculum, Ofsted can still exert considerable control over their choice of curriculum through its system of inspection. For example, the 'Early Years Foundation Stage' (EYFS) rules — the notorious 'nappy curriculum for under-fives — actually *prevents* them teaching subject knowledge, such as reading, for more than a fraction of the school year. It prefers sandpits and creative expression. Teachers say the EYFS wastes their time on pointless paperwork, yet it has been imposed on independent schools as well as state schools. Many independent schools believe that this nationalisation of the 0-5 years curriculum is merely the first step in nationalising the whole thing.

Before 2003, new independent schools could be inspected after opening, so they could get up and running before Ofsted passed comment on them. Since then, however, they have been forced to register *before* they open — and the conditions that they have to agree to before they can become registered have become more and more onerous. Indeed, in just those few years, the bureaucratic hurdles have been ratcheted up to the point where the New Model School Company's first school, which operated from a church hall, would not now be able to open at all, as the premises did not have a dedicated sick room with its own bed and running water.

For anyone considering opening a new independent school now, the bureaucratic barriers to entry are so high as to put off all but the hardiest of spirits. Plainly this must change if we are to bring choice, diversity and innovation into the business of education.

Now the knives are out for people who are so fed up with the state system or the national curriculum that they educate their own children at home. There are 40,000 or more children educated at home, according to Ann Newstead, spokesperson for the home education group Education Otherwise. Nobody is really sure of the number, but it is enough to unnerve civil servants. It would of course make sense for groups of parents, with different expertise, to collaborate on the home education of their children, but then of course all the adults would have to have criminal records checks and childminding qualifications, and their homes would need sick bays and all the other paraphernalia that Ofsted insists on. The latest assault, coming through a review and a parliamentary committee, is the suggestion that families who educate their children at home are prime suspects for child abuse. Of course, the reality is that parents who invest years in home education for their children are often doing it to save them from harm, such as bullying at school. But politicians and officials have now successfully tainted the whole idea of home education. So much for the 'diversity agenda'.

Bypassing local councils
In fact, we should make it easier for people who want some alternative to the dead bureaucratic hand of Ofsted and Whitehall — and for existing state schools to provide what

their parents want, rather than what ministers and officials deem is best for them. Carswell and Hannan, in *The Plan*, argue that there should be no central control of schools and the curriculum at all. They would close down most of the Whitehall department and the local authorities, through which the education budget is channelled, and instead divide the bulk of it among head teachers in proportion to the number of children they could attract to their school. Instead of complicated funding rules, it would be a straightforward per capita grant to each school, though there would be supplements for special needs (such as schools with a high proportion of non-English speakers).

In effect, all schools would get Academy status and financial freedom — though they need other freedoms too, such as the power to choose their own hours and holidays in line with parents' wishes. With funding going straight from the Treasury to the schools according to a set formula, we can scrap the local education authorities, though no doubt local authorities will resist this, still believing they know best what is good for us. Most of the department in Whitehall could go too — though in that case, there are likely to be fewer people springing to its defence.

The next phase in this particular education plan would be to allow parents to move their children into non-state schools, and for the same per capita funding to go to the school of their choice. Then, the education budget would follow the wants of parents, not the dictates of ministers and officials. That would make choices and opportunities available to all parents that are currently available only to the wealthiest.

Examples from abroad
This mixture of state funding but diverse provision already

has a positive history in other countries. The District of Columbia, for example, provides per capita funding for parents who choose independent schools for their children — and indeed, many such schools have been set up by groups of parents and teachers to provide children with a refuge against the drug and violence culture that has been all too prevalent in the public system. A study by Andrew J Coulson of the Cato Institute found these independent schools to be much cheaper than their public counterparts. After three years, their pupils are two years ahead in reading, and further advanced in other critical subjects too.

The independent schools in the District of Columbia serve a population that is commonly poor and black. David Green believes that these are exactly the sorts of families who benefit most from a money-follows-the-child system. He argues too that the schools can break out of the bureaucratic mould and shape themselves to serve the particular needs of their population. This is not just something for the concerned middle classes. Instead of ministers forlornly trying to engage unresponsive parents with official 'home-school contracts', for example, in a properly diverse system schools might spring up in difficult areas that actually specialise in delivering education to pupils whose parents are unsupport-ive. This, as the District of Columbia has shown, is selection in its true sense — not schools that choose the brightest children, but schools that are right for the particular needs of their population, whatever they are.

The Swedish schools revolution
Sweden is another place where this system of state funding but diverse public and private provision has been adopted. Denmark and the Netherlands have had something like it for

decades, and Sweden decided to go down this route in 1991. The policy was controversial at first: Sweden has never had independent schools like those in the UK, and eroding the state's monopoly on public services was seen as a big step. But now the new system has shown its value, and commands such huge levels of parental and public support — over 90% parental approval rating, in fact — that no political party now wants to repeal it. Indeed, Social Democrat politicians who initially promised to repeal the system, now number among its most dedicated proponents.

In Sweden today, the public money allocated for the education of a child follows that child to a school chosen by the parents, even if it is in a different educational district and even if it is a private school. To receive this money, however, schools must agree to take students on a first-come-first-served basis — no academic selection — and is not allowed to make additional charges of any kind — no top-up fees. The result has been that 1,200 new schools have sprung up to meet the latent demand from parents and capture the funding available from the public sector. Some 17% of Sweden's schools are now these 'free schools' (compared to just 2% of UK schools with Academy status). At the upper school level, they now educate a third of Swedish children.

Though comparative achievement data in Sweden are weak, in areas where competition is strongest and large numbers of these new schools have been created — mostly in the cities such as Stockholm, Gothenburg and Mälmo, though they have sprung up everywhere — mathematics grades (to take one objective measure) have risen fastest. And everyone agrees that even the municipal schools have improved under the threat of losing their tax-funded students to new independent schools.

The system has created real, genuine diversity too — not just the bureaucratic idea of diversity that some Whitehall mandarin might have in mind. The International English School, for example, has around 600 pupils and works from a science park north of Stockholm, renting its facilities in order to keep overheads down. It is one of a chain of fourteen new schools (of which Burnley-born Peter Fyles is the managing director); it uses internet technology to allow parents to access their child's attendance records, had a dedicated academic and personal counselling centre, and even offers GCSEs among its course qualifications.

A UK schools revolution

The first step in creating a similar revolution in the UK would be to empower parents to move their child to any state school in the country, and for the cost of a state education to follow that child to the new school. State schools themselves should be freed from local education authority control and allowed to pursue this source of funding as they deem fit. (This is one thing that really needs to be decided at the centre. Leaving it up to school ballots means that all the local bureaucrats will gang up to intimidate and alarm parents at one school after another; and leaving the decision to local authorities is *not* likely to lead to *any* changes.)

The ownership of state schools need not change, just as the municipal schools in Sweden are still owned by the municipality. However, as in Sweden, they would probably be much keener to raise their performance and enhance their offering in order to prevent an exodus of students to independent schools. As the new funding system gets established, though, it should be possible for parents and teachers to buy out the state's interest in the premises, and to establish their school as a fully independent 'free school', financed by the per capita grant paid by the state for each pupil it attracts.

This freedom would also have the additional benefit that it would motivate successful schools to expand. At present there is no reason at all why the head and management team of a successful state school should take over the running of a failing school nearby. It just means more headaches, without any additional administrative support. But we need a system in which successful and popular schools expand and absorb the unsuccessful ones.

Of course, the per capita state funding needs to be available to new schools as well, as it is in Sweden. This needs a radical clearing out of the regulations on what schools should look like (the sick bay example again) and how they should operate (such as the national curriculum). Planning rules need to be easier too: the government must get tough on local authorities using planning obstructions to prevent competition with their own local schools.

Likewise, the producer argument that popular schools should not be allowed to expand because there are still unfilled places at unpopular ones, should be consigned to the past. The whole point is to get fresh thinking into education, and to allow people to explore new and better ways of delivering the service. For that, you need to make it easy for new schools to start up, perhaps starting small — like the New Model School Company, many new Swedish schools started life renting spare rooms in community halls or office blocks — and then getting established, and expanding. Indeed, Denmark actually encourages parents and teachers to start up new schools if they feel they can do better than the government-run alternatives.

Why we need for-profit schools

The Conservatives have been as spineless as usual on the question of whether the new schools that receive per capita funding from the state should be allowed to make a profit. They have suggested that school buildings should be owned by charities, but that the operators who run them might just, possibly, be able to run for profit, maybe, perhaps, in the fullness of time. The Swedes, however, have no problem with this at all. About three quarters of Sweden's free schools are profit making — but if they take the government's money, they are not allowed to charge a fee. They cannot even make parents pay for field trips and sports equipment. So where is the problem?

According to Anders Hutin, one of the main designers of the Swedish reforms, the possibility of making a profit is in fact a crucial part of Sweden's success. For-profit schools see every pupil as a potential new source of income, and expand their capacity to absorb them. Non-profits, however, tend not to expand sufficiently, because long waiting lists are their criterion and mark of success. If you want the free school idea to spread, the schools have to be allowed to make profits. And many Swedish school providers achieve that by running not just one, but a chain of schools, pooling much of the administrative cost in a dedicated back office, and thereby are able to operate much more cheaply and with less duplication.

The need for information

Some people in the UK oppose any Swedish-style open access system because they believe that parents are too unmotivated or poorly informed to select the best school for their offspring. The obvious reality is quite different: parents go to great lengths to get their children into the schools they think are best for them — which might not always be the highly academic alternatives. Indeed, Anders Hutin believes that the UK is one of the countries best placed to benefit from a system based on the reforms in Sweden, given the high demand for good schools and the lengths to which parents here will go to secure a place in them.

Where there is no real choice, there is no point in spending time ferreting out information on individual schools, since it would not make any difference; so we should not be surprised if parents are indeed poorly informed today. Where there is diversity and choice, however, checking the alternatives makes every sense, and in the new system it is likely that parents will be much more deeply engaged in finding out which schools are best for their children, and in taking a keener interest in how schools are run.

Nevertheless, it may well be that some parents remain uninvolved in their kids' education, and unwilling to bother much about it, as many are today. But the benefits of this open access system accrue to their children just as much as to those of the most informed and pushy parents. As in Sweden, the mere threat that some parents could desert, or set up their own schools, is enough to bid up standards in the state sector — which helps everyone, even those who stay.

And it only takes a few informed students to make that difference for everyone. In the early 1990s, my son's school used the 'real books' method for reading. The kids just went to the bookshelf and took home any book they liked the look of. So there was no progression — they would take hard books home one week, easy ones the next, and by the time they saw a word the second time round, they had already forgotten it. We thought he needed more structured reading, so we moved him to another school — as one then could — which provided that. Within days, other parents, worried by the same issue, asked how we did it. Within weeks, a few more had joined us. Within a month, the school had held a crisis meeting and completely revamped the way it taught reading. Choice is a wonderful thing.

Plainly, if parents are to make choices within the new Swedish-style system, we would want them to have access to the most comprehensive information on the ethos, approach and achievements of different schools. As with the idea of putting government spending online, all that is necessary is for the government to publish the data in an open way, so that other people — local newspapers, for example, or consultants, or parent–teacher associations — can monitor, analyse, and present the data in ways that are accessible and useful to parents. Then, at last, it will be parents, not national and local politicians and civil servants, who will be in charge of how their children are taught.

Universities
Our universities need to be dragged away from the smothering bosom of the public sector too.

They used to say of Adam Smith, the Scottish philosopher whose 1776 book *The Wealth of Nations* created what we now call the science of economics, that he was the last man who knew everything. And it is almost true. He amassed a huge library on science, literature, the arts and philosophy, covering just about everything that was known in that memorable age.

But Adam Smith was not quite the last. Terence Kealey would do well on *Mastermind*. He is a modern-day polymath who also knows everything — or certainly seems to. A former Cambridge microbiologist and now head of the independent University of Buckingham, he can talk with knowledge, enthusiasm and enlightenment on any subject you care to name. The legacy of Alexander the Great today? Byzantine political and administrative systems? The evolution of lice? Why the Elizabethan statesman Francis Bacon was a crook? How the seventeenth century Dutch Republic became so rich so fast? Radio astronomy? The career of Lyndon B Johnson? He knows the lot.

As Kealey says in his Adam Smith Institute briefing paper *Transforming Higher Education* — and he should know — the best universities in the world are the independent universities in America. That is partly because they are able to spend up to five times more than universities here, thanks to their exploitation of private funding. We too need to get more private funding into higher education.

We have taken the first correct step by allowing universities to charge fees to students — of around £3,500, though this is only a fraction of the real cost of providing a university education — and instituting a loan system so that able students even of limited means should still have access. Kealey would go further and abolish the central university funding system entirely. Some of the money it gets would still be earmarked for research activities. The rest would go to the Student Loans Company (SLC) to increase its budgets for grants and loans. The SLC would become the Needs Blind Admissions Agency (NBAA): universities would admit students on merit, and the NBAA would cover the fees of those who could not afford to pay. That is exactly how the top American universities work — except that the student support money comes out of their hefty private endowments.

Kealey would allow UK universities to increase their fees to economic levels — which would be many times today's — but only as fast as they could build up their own endowments to make sure that no student is turned away because of an inability to pay. That is a huge task, but worth it to produce a system that puts a lot more money into academic achievement but simultaneously ensures that no bright but needy student is left out.

Channelling the state's contribution through the students who need help, rather than using it simply to subsidise the institutional providers, would give much greater freedom to our universities and would encourage more private giving. Again Kealey's polymath mind shows through when he talks about the Royal National Lifeboat Institution (RNLI), which was created independently in 1824, but fell on hard times thirty years later. In 1854 it accepted £2,000 a year in government grants. But with every pound the government put in, it lost well over a pound in voluntary donations. People just could not see why they should support a state-funded institution. So in 1869 the RNLI cut loose — and has flourished ever since. Today it is the twelfth-largest charity in the UK, running 320 lifeboats and rescuing some 6,000 people a year, and making our coasts safer than any that are maintained by other government's coastguards. Kealey is in no doubt that it is time for our universities to cut loose too.

7

HEALTHCARE

OPENING UP THE DOUBLE MONOPOLY

The National Health Service (NHS) is the world's biggest publicly funded health provider. Its funding comes directly from taxpayers and has doubled in real terms since 1997: it now stands at just over £100 billion, roughly £1,675 for every man, woman and child in the country. Today we spend more of our GDP on healthcare than the European average.

Around half of the extra spending has gone into higher wages rather than improvements in services, and now around 60% of the NHS budget goes on wages. Some eighty NHS executives earn more than the prime minister, but even family doctors can earn £100,000 or more and, thanks to the 'out of hours' terms of a generous contract hastily agreed by the former health secretary John Reid, still be on the golf course all weekend. In total, the NHS employs more than 1,500,000 people, including 90,000 hospital doctors, 35,000 family doctors (general practitioners, GPs), 40,000 nurses and 16,000 ambulance staff. It is said that only China's army, India's railways, and America's Wal-Mart corporation employ more people.

The NHS is run by the Department of Health (DH), which works through ten Strategic Health Authorities (SHAs) to plan the NHS's activities. The specific services are commissioned, and partially provided, through 147 Primary Care Trusts (PCTs) in England — Scotland, Wales and Northern Ireland have their own systems. There are 482 large hospitals and an even greater number of clinics and smaller units in the UK. Each week, around four million people will use some part of the NHS — about 90% of them just visiting their GP, through 700,000 visiting an NHS dentist, to 3,000 having a heart operation.

The disease

Yet despite its gee-whizz scale and the flash flood of new money, the NHS has serious problems. NHS services have not improved anything like as fast as its budget has grown. Indeed, its productivity has fallen. Some 44 NHS Trusts are actually in debt, and the number failing on core standards is rising. In November 2009 a study by the respected health information company Dr Foster found 27 hospitals with unusually high death rates, and twelve hospitals 'significantly underperforming' — having appalling surgical standards — despite eight of them being rated 'good' or 'excellent' by the official ratings quango, the Care Quality Commission.

According to Nick Seddon in his 2009 Civitas report *Quite Like Heaven?*, huge variations in service still exists: patients wait just three days for a CT scan at University College London Hospital, while at Norfolk and Norwich University Hospital they wait as much as four months. NHS bosses reckon that a quarter of patients in hospital do not need to be there. The middle classes can play the system, while the poor, mentally ill and ethnic minorities get a worse service. Hugely expensive equipment and facilities lie unused during the night and at weekends. The demands of patients cannot be met, more services are rationed and more patients are denied treatment. A quarter of a million people still wait more than 18 weeks for treatment. Waste and bureaucracy are legendary, and staff — now that the flash flood of money is over — are becoming demoralised once again.

The 2009 Euro Health Consumer Index (EHCI) placed the UK only 14th out of 33 countries in terms of the quality of its healthcare, citing its long waiting lists and uneven delivery of service. Only four countries in Western Europe did worse — Italy, Spain, Greece and Portugal. Meanwhile, a 2009 review by the US-based Commonwealth Fund found that in terms of deaths from treatable disease, the UK now ranks only tenth in Europe — and is continuing to slide. People are more than twice as likely to die of a heart attack in the UK than across the Channel in France. Our rates of survival from breast cancer were in the bottom quarter of European countries, while deaths from lung disease are 75% higher than the European average. Of the 200,000 people in the UK who die from cancer and strokes each year, 20,000 or more would survive if they lived anywhere else in northern Europe. (Just 15 of England's NHS trusts match Europe's highest cancer survival rates, and even the government's own director of cancer services, Professor Mike Richards, estimated that up to 10,000 people die needlessly every year because their cancer is diagnosed too late.) Meanwhile, around 5,000 people each year die from infections that they pick up while in an NHS hospital.

The idea of keeping the NHS as a highly centralised nationalised industry, whose problems could be solved by a little reorganisation, has plainly been tested to destruction. Equally though, planned moves to introduce more market-style principles into the Services have been faltering and half-hearted. A 'payment by results' system is supposed to steer NHS funding to the most effective NHS providers, much as a market would: but according to Seddon it is really only a 'payment by activity' scheme, with no link to actual health outcomes. Nor is there any real negotiation on payment rates as there would be in a market: in the NHS the so-called 'tariff' for various procedures is set centrally, sometimes so low that NHS providers actually lose money by doing them. Patients are supposed to have a choice between different NHS providers such as hospitals, but only around two-fifths of them (43%) recall being offered one. Although over 8,000 NHS patients now have their procedures done in private hospitals each month (including about a quarter of hip and knee replacements), only 6% of NHS spending is outsourced to non-NHS providers. Not choice, but centrally imposed targets remain the priority, even at the expense of clinical judgement — leading to perverse situations such as patients being left outside in ambulances because to admit them into Accident & Emergency (A&E) suites would jeopardise the all-important waiting time target.

The diagnosis
The NHS is too big to manage, and the reason for this is that nowhere else in Europe does such a high proportion of health spending come through the state. That spending comes, naturally enough, at the price of central political and bureaucratic control, with its constant top-down directives and re-*dis*organisations. The cold evidence from other European countries, perhaps Switzerland and the Netherlands in particular, is that it is possible to deliver comprehensive healthcare to everyone, at much higher standards, for the

same cost.

They do that, says Seddon, by harnessing the potential of real competition between service providers and real choice for service users. In neither system is government the main provider, or the main funder: its role is rather to regulate the delivery of healthcare.

This is not to say that UK healthcare has to be completely privatised. The difference between the UK and other, more successful, European countries is not just how much more they spend privately, and how much of their service is delivered by state organisations, but how much choice and variety there is in their funding and provision arrangements.

In this contest, Bismarck clearly beats Beveridge. Our system goes back to a plan drawn up by William Beveridge in the 1940s, in which funding and provision are organised by a single body — the NHS. By contrast, in Europe's Bismarck-style systems, going back to the nineteenth century German Chancellor Otto von Bismarck, funding is done by a multitude of social insurance organisations, and provision is done independently by another multitude of providers. Beveridge-style systems can be made to work in smaller countries, where the smaller scale makes them easier to manage, but otherwise it is Bismarck-style systems that occupy the higher places in the EHCI ratings: the Netherlands, Austria, Switzerland, Germany, France, Luxembourg and Belgium, all of them well ahead of the UK.

Snake oil cures
The UK public are so committed to the values of the NHS — healthcare delivered equitably, comprehensively and largely free at the point of use — that they believe they have to defend and maintain the Beveridge-style principles by which

it is organised. Yet the same values are perfectly compatible with Bismarck-style systems, which have the added benefit of delivering better results.

Hence the Conservatives' constant expressions of commitment to the NHS, and their suggestion that it is only its bloated bureaucracy that holds it back from delivering the world's best healthcare. (They say they can cut the cost of NHS bureaucracy by a third, from £4.5 billion to £3 billion, in just four years. Well, good luck with that one: perhaps the 'forces of conservatism' will roll over this time.) Local pay bargaining, they say, will allow local efficiency deals to spring up, cutting costs. (So they might, and it is ridiculous to pay the same wages in different parts of the country where the cost of living varies widely; but there will be enormous union resistance to sacrificing that particular principle.) And, they say, giving the NHS an independent board would depoliticise it and let it get on with the job of making us well. (Or it might instead just create the biggest unelected and unaccountable quango in the UK.)

The Conservatives have also maintained that they would spare the NHS budget from any budget cuts. This might play well among voters, but as a policy it is wrong. Firstly, the NHS bureaucracy needs some of the same belt-tightening that people in the private sector have endured, and that nearly all other Whitehall departments are going to have to go through. Secondly, healthcare is such a huge spending item that ring-fencing its budget inevitably means even more savage cuts. Conservative leaders have mentioned the figure of 10% cuts in other departments; but the rising cost of healthcare (a growing and ageing population, expensive new medical technologies, medicines and the rest) means that the NHS budget would have to grow at more than 2% in real terms just to stand still. Upping the NHS budget by 2%, thinks the Treasury, might create the need for cuts more like 20% in other departments. That will not be a pretty sight.

Cures worse than the disease

Tim Montgomerie is a Conservative thought entrepreneur. He set up and is one of the main contributors to the hugely influential and busy website *Conservative Home*, through which Conservatives all over the UK propose, analyse, debate and shape policy ideas. However much his Party might want to see the NHS budget ring-fenced, he agrees that this simply cannot be achieved in the present financial climate. If we want more spending on healthcare, maybe we have to fund it in a radically different way.

'I don't believe that a universal, taxpayer funded, free-at-the-point-of-use health service is sustainable,' he says. The demands on a free service simply grow and grow, particularly since we are all getting older and less willing to put up with illness and discomfort. He says the unsustainability of the free system is 'especially true in the context of the financial crisis. Given that healthcare accounts for about seventeen percent of public spending, no government that is serious about balancing the books can afford to ring-fence it, as the Tories currently propose.' The NHS budget simply *has* to be trimmed; and it is only by getting more choice and competition into both the funding and the delivery of healthcare that this can be done without sacrificing performance.

One thing is for sure, though: nobody wants to copy the American model. True, it delivers the world's highest standard of healthcare — but at huge cost. Based around private insurance plans, critics often describe it as an example of capitalist greed writ large, and point to 46 million Americans being uninsured and denied treatment. But this is a caricature. In fact, America spends far more in total on providing free medical care than the UK does. The system is not a free market at all, but is ruthlessly regulated by the states. Sometimes that means insurance companies being forced to provide expensive Rolls-Royce services, even if customers simply want a Ford Focus level of protection. As for the 'uninsured Americans', well, nearly 10 million of them are not US citizens, 14 million are eligible for free healthcare services and would certainly be treated if they turned up in A&E, nearly 18 million earn more than $25,000 and probably figure they can pay for most things out of pocket, and just over 18 million are under 34 and reckon they do not need health insurance anyway.

Many parts of the US healthcare system deliver much better value for money than does the NHS. Kaiser Permanente, a 'health maintenance organisation' originally founded in 1933 to provide healthcare to workers on the Colorado River Aqueduct, has almost nine million members. Its family premium, at just over $13,000, is more, but not hugely more, than the NHS spends on a family here. The difference is that Kaiser members can see a doctor with hardly any wait at all, have access to specialists in days rather than months, and have far better medical outcomes than the average in the UK.

The real shortcoming in American healthcare is not that it is based around private insurance, but that the insurance is based around workplaces. Since employers pay for it, trade unions campaign to make it as comprehensive and generous as possible — but insuring everything down to a sticking plaster — sorry, a Band-Aid — is hugely expensive: the administrative cost is much more than the cure itself. And again, since employers are paying, workers tend to volunteer for every test and treatment that is going, egged on of course by the doctors who will get paid for it. Another shortcoming is that when people leave their job, they lose their insurance until they can get another job; and when they do start new jobs their existing health problems will put up the cost of their insurance, or reduce the coverage available to them. If America instead had an insurance system based around individuals — a lifetime protection plan, with the government paying the premiums for those who were out of work or otherwise unable to pay — it would have far fewer problems and far lower costs.

Exploring other cures

If America's convoluted, over-regulated insurance system is not right for the UK, then what else is feasible? Since roughly 90% of the contact that people in the UK have with the NHS is at the GP level, perhaps we should start there. GPs are already technically independent — though it is the government which decides how much they will be paid, and the NHS which decides how they should work.

Pointing out that the government spends nearly £20 billion on primary care services (not just GP surgeries, but clinics and dentists too), Tim Montgomerie says he would privatise the lot of them. 'Clinicians should offer their services in a free, competitive market,' he says. 'Patients would be free to shop around and would then pay directly for any services. Of course, an NHS entitlement could still be available for those unable to pay their own way. Britain's high street opticians — Specsavers, Vision Express and the like — provide a good example of how this could work in practice.'

Indeed they do. When opticians were closely regulated by the health authorities and competition between them was weak and rather genteel, eye tests and spectacles cost a lot more money, the process took a lot more time, and the choice of frames and services was a lot less. But competition reigns now that regulation has been eased, and that has been good for customers. Perhaps Tim is right: as long as we can ensure that people on low incomes or those with chronic conditions are not disadvantaged, it is now time to deregulate the family doctoring business.

Doctors curing doctors

And what of the rest of the system? How can we focus that more on the wants and needs of the patients, rather than the producers? Well, there are many ways, but all of them involve something more Bismarck-style than we have at the moment — indeed, something quite similar to the education reforms in Sweden. Instead of the budget filtering down from the Treasury through layer upon layer of NHS bureaucracy, and instead of provision being rigidly controlled through a pyramid of power descending from Downing Street, the solution is to have patients themselves given control over how their bit of the government's health budget is spent, and to allow them to spend it on any of a multitude of providers, as they deem fit.

There is, of course, a knowledge problem. Most people with a medical condition do not necessarily know how best to cure it — though with the millions of internet health pages and patient groups, that is certainly changing. They almost certainly will not know which are the best doctors and the best hospitals to treat them and care for them. So if, like

Swedish parents, they are to make a choice, they need good advice. Some years ago, David Green of Civitas suggested setting up a number of advisory groups, whose function was to advise patients how to shop around in a more market-style system. And there are of course the Bismarck models, where people can choose between competing social insurance funds.

Probably the easiest option for the UK, however, is to give the bulk of the health budget to GPs, and let them spend it buying in whatever healthcare services that they and their patients deem appropriate. GPs are, after all, the people to whom we all go when we are seeking advice about our health. We trust their judgement on our treatment, and they are the ones who set things up for us if we need to see a specialist or go into hospital. The drawback is that GPs also provide a growing number of healthcare services themselves, and it is generally a bad idea to put someone who wants to have your money in charge of spending it. But at least the UK has some experience of managing such a system. Before it was all unwound by the Old Labour health secretary Frank Dobson in 1997, roughly half the UK's family doctors had become 'fundholders' — that is, they controlled their patients' bit of the NHS budget and bought in services with it on their behalf. With the GPs acting as keen and knowledge-able customers, the result was that patients had to wait less time for consultant appointments and hospital admissions, there was greater efficiency and cost-consciousness among consultants and hospitals and — according to Professor Julian LeGrand of the London School of Economics — an overall rise in NHS productivity which peaked in 1997 and fell fast thereafter.

'So why not move to 100% GP fundholding?' asks Neil

O'Brien of Policy Exchange. 'GPs would simply be given control of the funds to buy in care for their patients, and could buy it in from anyone — NHS or private specialists and consultants, on an open market in healthcare provision.'

That way, patients would benefit from the competition among providers, whether they are independent or NHS providers. Even the modest volume of contracting out today has brought forward huge innovations in service provision. (One medical group, for example, used mobile operating theatres to go around the country and mop up long NHS waiting lists in place after place. Other providers are looking at nurse-led clinics on supermarket sites, like those pioneered by Wal-Mart in the US, of which there are now many hundreds.)

Because of competition and diversity in provision, patients in a GP fundholding system would also have more choice about what sort of treatment to have, rather than accepting the NHS orthodoxy; and in their GP, they would have an expert guide to navigate them through the options — one much closer to them, more objective, and more of a friend, than the present bureaucracy of the PCTs, who are in charge of buying in their treatment today, and indeed of supplying some of it. Moreover, just as in Sweden's education system, the public healthcare budget would be automatically and continuously steered to where the public, and not the politicians, thought it should be spent.

Self medication

GP fundholding could bring big improvements to the way the healthcare budget is spent, and is something we have experience of and which could implement very quickly. As it gets more established, though, we might indeed be able to go further and open up not just the provision of healthcare, but its funding too. Douglas Carswell and Daniel Hannan have proposed medical savings accounts, like those that prevail in Singapore and which are now growing in the United States; and I worked out the details of how this might function here in my 2002 Adam Smith Institute report *Why Not A Medical ISA?* Fundamentally, the idea is that the taxes which people pay towards the NHS are not put into one central pot administered by bureaucrats, but are saved into the patient's own medical fund. Those funds grow each year, and from them, patients can buy in whatever medical care they believe they need, putting them firmly in control. If they do not spend their whole fund, the surplus can be put towards other things, such as their retirement pension, or even paying off their mortgage. That, of course, encourages patients to seek value for money — something notoriously absent in America's insurance system, where patients are unconcerned about cost because their employers are paying.

However, health is more difficult to fund in this sort of way than education. While the cost of a school education is fairly predictable, the amount of medical treatment that someone might need during their life varies hugely. A savings vehicle alone may not be sufficient.

I have always thought that healthcare is one of those areas of life that is crying out for a businesslike partnership between the individual, private insurance, and the state. When you insure your car or your home, there is always an 'excess', meaning that small amounts are not covered. That makes good sense, because as with America's Band-Aids, the cost of administration would be more than the cost of the claim; insuring everything greatly raises the cost of insurance. So when you scratch your car, you do not claim on the insurance: you pop down to Halfords, buy a small pot of matching paint, and use your kid's watercolour brush to cover it up. When you crash into a bollard — well, then it might be worth making a claim.

Health should work the same way. Most people could pay for small medical expenses themselves. Indeed, for things like cough and cold remedies, most people already do. A medical savings account system might help more people to be able to save for a wider variety of comparatively small treatments.

Above that, there is a role for insurance. Insurance is no good for very small items, nor for things that people would willingly choose to have, like breast implants or in-vitro fertilisation (IVF), nor for things that you know for sure are going to happen to you. But it is great for things that are costly, nasty and unpredictable — if you develop appendicitis or kidney stones, for example, and need to go into hospital for treatment.

There are, however, many conditions that insurers find it hard to cover, because the uncertainties and long-term costs are just so great. Kidney disease, for example, may demand years of dialysis or an expensive transplant operation and all the aftercare that goes with it. The time that people might spend in a residential care home, similarly, may run into years, and the bills can run into hundreds of thousands. These things do not take naturally to insurance; but here there is a case for the state covering the financial gap.

A complete recovery
Indeed, this kind of three-way partnership could solve much of the increasing problem we have today regarding social care. When medical care is free, but social care is not, all

sorts of boundary problems occur. Scotland has chosen to rub out the boundary by paying for social care out of taxation, but the future costs of this, particularly given the ageing population, are astronomic. Few politicians, and perhaps not many taxpayers, want to contemplate that cost.

Through a partnership arrangement, however, such items are just as easily dealt with as medical care would be. People could be asked to insure themselves for an average time in a care home, for example — which would be affordable — with the state paying the costs if the person needed to stay longer. Here again, we would be extending the private sector into the areas it is good at, and using state finance only where it is necessary. The Conservatives' alternative — people pay the government £8,000 and the government gives them free social care — is merely an extension of state social insurance. And as an insurance company, the state sucks.

Eventually, I am sure, we will have to move to a healthcare system based around an individual-insurance-state partnership, with ISA-style health savings accounts for the first bit of that and competing private insurance for the second. The system in the Netherlands, though not perfect, might provide a model. For most short-term medical treatment, they have a system of compulsory insurance, with competing companies providing a government-defined package of services. If people cannot afford insurance, the state pays on their behalf, but people are free to purchase additional coverage (such as dentistry or physiotherapy). Equality of access is maintained by the simple rule that insurers have to take anyone who applies, and the premiums are the same for everyone, regardless of their age or their health condition. Half the cost comes from payroll taxes and a little more from government grants, so individuals end up paying about £90 a month.

Like the insurance companies, hospitals in the Netherlands are mostly privately run, and run for profit. This gives patients all the benefits of having a dynamic, competitive market in healthcare provision. Patients choose which hospital and treatment they feel is right for their own particular circumstances, and there is a growing volume of information on the internet to help them make that choice. If you are dissatisfied with your insurer or your providers, you can simply switch. Why should it not be possible to give patients the same sort of market power over their healthcare in the UK?

8

WELFARE

IDLE HANDS

In the words of the Lionel Bart song, fings ain't wot they used to be. Just as well. A hundred years ago, a great aunt of mine ended up in a Shropshire cemetery at a very young age because she was imprudent enough to have a child even though she was not married. The shame of it, according to my uncle, was so profound that she went out of her mind and committed suicide.

Of course, it could have been that she was a bit flaky even before the event, and that this led her into a liaison that other people would have avoided, as being a sure source of subsequent embarrassment and distress. It is not uncommon; indeed, if you shake my family tree hard enough, quite a few shotgun pellets fall out of the branches.

Today, almost half the children in the UK are born to unmarried parents (a generation ago, only one in ten were); and a quarter are raised by a lone parent (compared to just one in six in the 1970s). Yet we are much more inclined to sympathise with the many difficulties faced by lone parents, rather than to regard them as shameful. So why, in the Edwardian era — and before and beyond — should being an unmarried mother have carried such stigma for my great aunt?

Perhaps her behaviour affronted the religious standards of the time. Yet when religious push comes to financial shove, it is more often the latter that prevails. The fact is that when men were the principal breadwinners and female jobs were generally menial and low-paid, having a child outside of a stable relationship caused problems not just for you but the whole of your family. Without any welfare benefits to help you, and with little prospect of earning enough for the two of you to live on, you became a burden on your parents, your aunts or your sisters. And that, of course, was deeply embarrassing all round.

Are we doing more harm than good?
I am certainly relieved that, outside the most deeply religious families, young girls today do not feel driven to suicide because of the shame of having a child with no resident male earner to support them. Yet while our benefit system has spared us some such evils, I cannot escape thinking that it has created many more. We now have a record 2.6 million people claiming to be unfit for any kind of work, for example. That cannot be due to falling health standards, because the nation's health and longevity has improved. Does it perhaps have more to do with the fact that you can stay on incapacity benefits for decades, and that civil servants do little to find out whether people's fitness has changed, or to find them alternative work that is within their capacity? That very few people on benefits of any kind lose them, even when they blatantly break the rules? How too do we explain the fact that one in seven working-age households depend on social benefits for more than half their income, when the nation as a whole has been getting more prosperous and when opportunities have never been greater?

Can the fact that we pay £75 billion a year to working-age adults and their children be unrelated to the fact that some six million people of working age live on out-of-work benefits? Or in term of single parenthood once again, is it purely coincidence that we have the highest proportion of single parents in the EU (and the highest teenage pregnancy levels), when the benefits we pay to single parents are also some of the highest in Europe — and when our benefit system makes 1.8 million couples better off by splitting up than they would be if they stayed together? Does the fact that child poverty is up, and that income inequality is higher than for three decades, indicate that we have too little social support, or that our benefits system — which two-fifths of all claimants believe would make them worse off if they worked more — is trapping people in poverty and unemployment? Is the fact that one in five of our young people are not in education, training or a job indicate that the £2 billion we spent on the New Deal was insufficient, or is it because too many young people grow up in environments in which three generations of their friends and relatives have lived on benefits, that they never actually meet anyone who has a job, and that they reckon that being out of work and on benefits is an easy option — or dispiritingly, their destiny?

Joblessness, lack of ambition, widening inequality between those in work and those on state support, lack of saving, indebtedness, family break-up, teenage pregnancy, a rise in lone parenthood, social dysfunctionality, perverse incentives, low ambitions, a declining acceptance of personal responsibility, bureaucracy, the erosion of family and community help networks, fraud and (as the former welfare minister Frank Field noted) people actually worsening their circumstances so that they qualify for benefits — yes, I think our benefits system has a lot to answer for.

A costly, bureaucratic quagmire

Yet we are drawing ever-larger numbers of people into this quagmire of perverse incentives. Benefits have been extended to more and more people, without any robust scrutiny system to control the numbers or to judge whether state support is really necessary for them. Like so many parts of the benefit system, Gordon Brown's tax credits were introduced for the best of reasons — to provide help and incentives to the working poor. But it has become a bureau-cratic black hole, sucking in the middle classes. At a time when the median gross wage is £21,320, some 300,000 people are being paid benefits in excess of £20,000. That is a number of people equivalent to the population of Cardiff or Coventry. And the number of people drawing more than £15,000 in benefits has doubled since 1997, to 1.2 million, a number of people comfortably larger than the entire population of Birmingham.

I learn why we have reached this situation from Richard Wellings, the deputy editorial director at the Institute of Economic Affairs (IEA) — the granddaddy of all the think tanks that promote the ideas of social and economic freedom. Richard is an unassuming, rigorous and thoughtful social economist. As well as his IEA work, he has also written papers for Policy Exchange and is a regular contributor to various blogs too. As we meet in Westminster, he reminds me of some of the problems that keep people trapped on benefits.

'For example, the child tax credit system,' he says, 'works to destroy family incentives. The benefits are generous — their inventor, Gordon Brown, wanted particularly to show that he was "supporting children" and "tackling child poverty" — and are paid to households whether they are in work or out of work. So families need a huge increase in wages, and to be earning a substantial amount, before they will ever break free of these benefits and the level of dependency that comes with them.'

Housing benefit is another problem that means that many people on benefits would have to earn an awful lot more before they would ever escape dependency on benefits. 'Over a quarter of housing benefit payments go to people in London,' Richard continues. 'Rents are of course particularly high in London, which means that people take a huge hit in their pocket when they start earning a little more and lose it. It is a huge disincentive against taking a job and a real barrier for those who simply want to improve life for their families.' He favours solutions that increase the supply of low-cost accommodation — such as reining back planning controls and building regulations — as well as ending the local authority housing policies that trap people in high-cost areas.

Whatever the sources of the benefits bear-trap, however, the cost of our state benefits system is as gargantuan as its bureaucracy. In 2009/10, taxpayers stumped up £19.6 billion for housing benefit; £15.7 billion for child tax credits; another £14.7 billion for income support; £11.8 billion on child benefit (most of which goes to middle-class, rather than poor, families). That is not to mention the £67.2 billion cost of the state pension.

The sheer bureaucratic complexity of the whole thing is also jaw-dropping. The official handbook on benefits runs to 1,784 pages, and the department for work and pensions published a further 8,690 pages of guidance help. There are at least 51 different benefits, and as tax lawyer David Martin points out in his 2009 Centre for Policy Studies report *Benefit Simplification*, there are different rules for different ones: how much you can earn and still draw them, how much of your savings are taken into account, how long they are paid for, whether they are calculated weekly or annually, and much more. Benefits overlap with one another; the same circumstances can entitle you to a range of different benefits; and one benefit entitles you to another, different set as well. As a claimant, you face a multitude of different forms to fill in, which is particularly off-putting for older people; once you have done your forms, different agencies will reach different decisions about your eligibility; and they will take their time about it, which is bad news if you are urgently needing help. Meanwhile, the complexity of the system hides a swamp of fraud and error. Not long ago, it was discovered that some two million poorer families received an average of £1000 in tax credit overpayments — which our ever-caring Revenue & Customs then demanded back from them immediately; around £400 million is overpaid each year in housing benefit; as for fraud, nobody has the foggiest, except that it is in the billions.

How we close off the work option
Trying to move off benefits and into work is a nightmare. Work (or try to improve your prospects by studying) for more than 16 hours a week and you lose income support, jobseeker's allowance and all the other benefits like free school meals that go alongside — which is why employers in some lines of work have so much trouble finding people to work a full shift, and instead have to hire two or three part-timers, with all the paperwork that involves. Worse, the claimants themselves remain trapped in low-paid, part-time

work, their only route to self-improvement barricaded off to them.

If you take a job, you not only face taxes, but you lose benefits — which might well make you think it is not worth the effort. It almost certainly would not be if your household income was little more than £5,000, because for every extra £1 you earned, you could well lose over 95p, leaving you with less than 5p to take home. Earn about £6,000 and you lose about 85p; then at about £7,500 you are losing 90p again. In fact, some 60,000 households lose 90p or more for every extra £1 they earn — if, indeed, they bother. Far more, around 2 million working people, lose over 60p on every extra £1 they earn. You have to earn about £31,000 before you actually get to keep more than you lose.

Taking into account what you pay to Revenue & Customs and what you lose in benefits, the upshot is that the very poorest people in the country are paying the highest effective tax rates. People can even *lose money* by working — and I do not mean just because of your extra travel or clothing costs. An unemployed couple on jobseekers' allowance get £100.95 a week. The Centre for Social Justice's calculations show that if one of them took a part-time, minimum-wage job, their income would *fall* by £9.27. Even working thirty hours a week would make them only £41.33 better off. Would *you* want to work for just £1.38 an hour?

It's absolutely bonkers. Indeed, it is criminal, and the politicians and officials who have come up with this discouraging, soul-destroying, motivation-mangling mess should all be in jail serving time for totally fouling up people's lives.

Clearing the route to self-help
The trouble is that our benefits system focuses entirely on

trying to raise the level of household income (though as I have said, it does this in a mindlessly complex, haphazard and perverse way). What it does not bother about is whether that income comes through work or from benefits. Yet the government's own research shows that the *source* of a household's income is actually more important than the *level* of income. A system that penalises work, as ours does, and focuses on how much income people have without seeing the difference between earnings from work and earnings from benefits, merely attacks the *symptoms* of poverty, dependency and social exclusion.

As the Centre for Social Justice's excellent 2009 report *Dynamic Benefits* rightly concludes, such a system is counterproductive and must be reformed. We need instead to understand the *dynamic* effects of benefits, and of work — and to build afresh a welfare system that supports and promotes *work* as the only positive, humane, enduring route out of poverty. Gordon Brown's tax credits were a grossly over-engineered and wasteful stab at that. We need instead to drastically reduce the barriers to benefit claimants entering work and earning more; and (as Corin Taylor of the Institute of Directors put it to me) to increase the supply of 'starter' jobs by greatly reducing the regulation, taxes and paperwork that prevents employers creating new jobs. We could start by eliminating national insurance, and all the paperwork that goes with it, on small companies.

To create this positive dynamics, the Centre for Social Justice propose a radical simplification of benefits, down from 51 to just two — a work credit for those out of work or on very low wages (replacing jobseekers' allowance, employment and support allowance, income support and incapacity benefit); and a life credit (to cover additional expenses such as housing, council tax, disability expenses and family needs).

Now we are getting somewhere. The next step is to make sure that beneficiaries who do try to flesh out their household income by going to work do not lose their benefits in quite such a spectacular manner. If people do not get to keep at least a third — or better, more than half — of what they get paid from work, it is quite understandable that they would be reluctant to leave benefits. Doing that, of course, means looking at the tax system and the benefits system together, and maybe moving towards a so-called negative income tax, whereby people earning good money pay tax, and people on lower incomes get cash back. At the very least, we need to radically increase the 'earnings disregards': the amount of money you can earn and still draw benefit at the same time. The Centre for Social Justice would raise the amount to £3,500 and beyond. While we are at it, we need to get rid of the absurdity where couples are better off if they split.

We should also end the situation where through housing benefit we support people to rent a home but not to buy one — adding to insecurity and not promoting saving in the slightest. Indeed, the whole benefit structure should be a lot simpler. When you go for a job, your employer does not ask how many children you have to support, or where you live and whether you are renting or buying — you are paid the rate for the job. State welfare should be simple too. State bureaucracies are not very good at dealing with complex individual needs — charities, community and voluntary groups do the job much better. The state should stick to the simple things and encourage others to step in where it leaves gaps to be filled. Boil it all down to a single benefit form that goes to one single benefit office that comes up with one

single decision on eligibility, and you have taken out a huge
wodge of complexity, bureaucracy, cost and perversity.

Rights and responsibilities

Job done? Well not quite, because we need to encourage the
people who could haul themselves off benefits to do so, not
just by financial incentives but by moral suasion too. After
all, suppose your brother lost his job and you agreed to help
him out with a monthly cheque. If after a couple of months
he showed no sign of doing anything to get a new job and
seemed content to live off your generosity forever, most
people would think it perfectly right that you should have a
frank word with him, and indeed stop your subsidies to him
if he is still sitting at home watching TV all day. It should be
no different with state benefits — though the moral
dimension comes more naturally in a relationship between
siblings, or between a needy person and a charitable or
voluntary group, than between the state and its beneficiaries.
The state is driven by rules, not moral relationships: it is just
too clunky for that.

Even so, many countries have tried to make their state
benefits conditional on the recipients doing at least
something to try to get themselves off benefits and into work.
Our own New Deal, introduced by Gordon Brown in 1997
and reinvented several times since, was an attempt to do that,
demanding that young people should be in work, or
education, training or voluntary work, and that there would
be no fifth option of life on benefits. Naturally it has never
worked, being mired in Brown's culture of central bureaucratic control.

Yet *conditionality*, as it is called, can work and does work
in many parts of the globe, even those like Sweden and

Norway that are thought of as deeply committed to the principles of a welfare state. Indeed, even President Clinton signed up to the principle in 1996, with the Personal Responsibility and Work Opportunity Reconciliation Act. (American legislators *do* choose pompous names for their laws; but at least they tell you what the measure is about — unlike things such as the Terrorism Act in the UK, which is more often used to allow councils to spy on people's wheelie-bin habits, rather than to thwart bombers.) After the 1996 law, US welfare caseloads fell by around two-thirds in just five years — over 8 million people moving off benefits and, mostly, into work.

Dr Oliver Marc Hartwich is very thorough when it comes to facts, figures and the details of public policy options. But then he is German. He also has a Master's degree in business and economics and a doctorate in law. Fed up with the general nannying and intrusiveness of the German state, he had hoped to make his life in the good old liberal UK. He did a spell as adviser to the LibDem peer and finance spokesman Lord Oakeshott, and went on to become chief economist at Policy Exchange, where he published a string of impressive reports on housing, planning, transport and much else. Unfortunately he discovered that, despite its liberal history and tradition, the UK was now even less liberal than Germany, so he packed his bags and went off to Australia, to work with the excellent policy entrepreneur Greg Lindsay at the Centre for Independent Studies in Sydney.

Australia, he tells me, is another country that has cut its welfare roles by simple conditionality — or 'mutual obligation' measures as they are known. When benefit claimants were asked to turn up for an interview to assess their case and discuss what sort of work they might be capable of doing, around five or ten percent of them dropped off the rolls. But then about five or ten percent of them already had black market jobs that they were not declaring, or were perfectly willing to live off the income of a partner. Ask them to actually turn up to a job training programme and another third figure they do not actually need social benefits and can get a job on their own. Australia's job training strategy does seem to be effective (much more so than America's). A 2004 survey showed that half the Australians who had moved off benefits and into work thought that these programmes and other mutual obligation requirements of their benefits had been important or useful in helping them.

Oliver's native Germany introduced a 'rights and respon- sibilities' culture into its benefits system, he says in the 2009 Policy Exchange report *When Hassle Means Help*, which he edited along with the think tank's research fellow Lawrence Kay. 'Claimants saw that receiving benefits did not mean life on state money without any responsibility,' he says. 'This change was the driving force behind reforms that helped cut Germany's unemployment rolls from 5 million to 3.5 million in just two years.'

Sweden, that traditional welfare paradise, has also been quietly raising the responsibilities of beneficiaries. Since 2000, they have to be available for and actively seeking work. They also have to consider jobs of different kinds and to consider jobs outside their community, if the travel time is reasonable. As Corin Taylor of the Institute of Directors put to me, as well as making it more worthwhile for people to leave benefits and get into work, it is also vital to encourage employers, particularly small firms, to create the new job opportunities for them. Sweden's government also thinks on these lines, and has made it cheaper and easier for firms to hire new employees, particularly newly arrived refugees and people who have been unemployed for a long time.

In Norway too, work requirements and job training programmes are widespread, which again has increased the probability of people moving off benefit and into work. And in Switzerland, each canton designs its own local welfare programme — keeping things local and decentralised seems to be a key feature of successful welfare reforms around the world — but in general, only people in work are eligible for most benefits.

Benefits in Switzerland, and in Sweden, are also time limited, which concentrates the mind: a lot more people start taking jobs when their benefit is about to expire. America's benefits are also time limited, with a lifetime limit of five years. Studies show that this has been a major cause of the dramatic drop in the welfare rolls there. But of course any such limit has to be balanced with active programmes to help people into work.

America's welfare reforms
Some places in America are quite good at this. The intelligent and personable Jason Turner used to work as a policy analyst for my brother Stuart at the Heritage Foundation in Washington DC. He is much better known, however, as the architect of Wisconsin's welfare-to-work programme — and then of New York's. This man is a serial reformer.

The Wisconsin Works (W-2) programme cut out the standard Federal benefit, Aid to Families with Dependent Children, and replaced it with cash help tied to participation in work-type activities. Beneficiaries were assigned a Financial and Employment Planner (FEB), who assessed their level of self-sufficiency and encouraged them to move up the ladder to greater independence. Small loans, repayable in cash *or* community service, were on offer to help people find work — so people could perhaps get a new suit of clothes for interviews, or fix their car so they could get to work — and there was childcare help too.

The programme focused on work rather than education, but there were activities such as improving interview skills, and community service. Beneficiaries on the lower rungs of self-sufficiency received a monthly grant, which was docked each time they failed to participate in the programmes. And there was counselling on the problems of dependency, and supervised job searches. The next stage of progress might be a state-sponsored job, or a full-time job in the private sector.

Because of the nature of welfare and employment, with people dropping in and out of them all the time, it is hard to be precise about the success of W-2, but the welfare rolls and the number of welfare applicants both fell sharply. And with its intensive mentoring and training programmes, it was not a cheap option. Still, mayor Rudi Giuliani wasted no time in poaching Jason Turner to do much the same in New York too. Again, the philosophy was that the best way to help people on welfare benefits — particularly those who do not understand or have the habits of work, like showing up regularly and on time — is to get them working *somewhere*, with a caseworker to make sure they get up and go to work every day.

New York also tackled beneficiaries who claimed to be unable to work, employing doctors and caseworkers to evaluate them. If the doctor concluded that a bad back or asthma, say, restricted what jobs someone could do, the caseworker would plan job searches on the basis of those problems. (In US surveys, even disabled people themselves seem to regard this as more positive than the old system.) In the first five years of the programme, between 1995–2000, New York's welfare caseload dropped by 54% — more than 1 million people — and by 2006, mayor Michael Bloomberg had cut the numbers by another 25%.

Lessons from the US experience

As Katherine Hirst explains in her 2007 Adam Smith Institute report *Working Welfare*, US welfare reformers make no bones about setting themselves the objective of cutting the number of people on the benefit rolls. A life on benefit, they argue, is corrosive: people lose the habits of work, become less employable, lose self-esteem, and get used to living a life near the poverty line. The best way out of poverty is to have a job, even a minimum-wage job, with the possibility of getting a better one. That is why reformers have focused on getting people off welfare and into work. To do that requires individual mentoring and support, with an emphasis on personal and parental responsibilities, tailored around the specific problems that close off job opportunities for people — illiteracy, lack of skills, addiction, family dysfunction, disabilities or even simple things like not having adequate means to get to work.

Large-scale national welfare systems cannot deliver that personal, intensive caseworker involvement. On the basis of the US experience, Katherine concludes that welfare programmes have to be designed and run by local people, so that they take account of local conditions and can be focused around individuals and their needs. There must, of course, be minimum national standards, particularly national standards for the treatment of disabled persons. Otherwise, the centre should simply give block welfare grants to the localities and let them decide how it should be used, and on things like how steeply benefits should be tapered out once people are in work.

Or indeed, non-state organisations can be brought in. In the UK, I would start by privatising the Jobcentre Plus network (it is Plus not because it does anything more than the old jobcentres did, but just to make politicians feel that they have invented something new: civil servants are very good at suggesting name changes to make them feel that). America goes further, though, relying on church and voluntary groups, charities and even private companies for the job of getting people off welfare and into work. They are smaller, lighter, nimbler, less rule-bound, more focused on the specific needs of the individuals, and better able to deal with circumstances that are personal, unique, and complicated than are large state bureaucracies. The focus has to be on work as the antidote to poverty, and the objective for these organisations must be not just to get people into work, but to get them into jobs they stick at. That is why American states that contract out case management to non-state agencies often do not pay out most of their contract money until the person under their care has managed to hold down a job for at least three months. After that length of time at least, there is a good chance that they will stay in employment.

For reforms to succeed, though, reducing the number of benefit dependents and getting people into work must be the target. Loans seem a better way of giving people the help they need to get back into work than are open-ended benefits; and people are more likely to get into work if benefits are time limited. Family networks are important too: US reformers insist that single mothers below 16 should not be eligible for benefit if they live at home, which they should generally be expected to do; and many would make it mandatory for fathers to be named on birth certificates, so that fathers could not escape their responsibility, something that is all too common in the UK. And personally, I would ask disabled groups to take charge of monitoring who was and was not genuinely able to do at least some form of work. Or for that matter, hand over the whole book to the management of a private insurer — who will do things like making sure that people actually get treatment for their problem before it turns into a life-ruining disability, and working out what jobs people can actually do within their physical and mental capabilities, and then getting them to do it. Then the taxpayer could just keep the change, which I figure would run into billions. When Labour was in opposition, its leaders always chided the Conservatives that two fifths of the incapacity benefit caseload amounted to 'disguised unemployment', though they seemed unable to get to grips with it themselves when in power. So there is some scope for savings there, I reckon.

If you are going to have a tax credit system to ensure that benefits do not taper off too sharply, and so encourage people to improve themselves in work, it should look more like America's simple Earned Income Tax Credit (EITC) rather than Gordon Brown's convoluted tax credit schemes. Indeed, family taxation needs a complete overhaul. We are so focused on income redistribution from rich families to poor families that we have forgotten the devastating effect of taxation *within* families. Brown's replacement of tax allowances for spouses and dependent children was a bad mistake, and the fact that millions of couples find themselves better off by splitting up is a social disaster. As

Christina Odone points out in her 2009 Centre for Policy Studies paper *What Women Want*, single-earner couples — one of those fings wot used to be the norm until quite recently — are actually made worse off by the tax system than couples who earn the same amount but in which both are working. David Green of Civitas makes the same point: couples should be able to share the burden of working and caring for children between themselves, he says, without having to worry about whether the tax system will make them better off in one arrangement and worse off in another. He favours the French system of a family tax allowance, whereby family members can apportion their incomes so as to minimise tax and share the parenting responsibilities as they think best. I think he is right.

Taking the poor out of taxation entirely

If getting people into work is the best anti-poverty strategy, taxing them as soon as they do earn much over £100 a week is not going to help. As the Nobel economist Milton Friedman wisely told me: 'If you pay people when they don't work, and tax them when they do, you're going to get unemployment.' But we could change that balance, and greatly boost the incentives for benefit claimants to get into a job and indeed get a better job, if we took poorer people out of tax entirely.

It is absolutely stark bonkers that people earning half the minimum wage should also be paying tax. Tax should be paid by people who can afford it — Adam Smith knew that and said as much more than 250 years ago, so by now this idea is hardly a breathtaking novelty. The minimum wage, which comes to about £12,000 for someone working full time, is by definition reckoned to be a pretty poor income — average earnings are about twice that. Yet people pay tax on every penny over £6,035. So we have to pay them social benefits to compensate. It is an absolutely bizarre way of doing things, and a grossly unfair one.

The solution is simple. 'People on the minimum wage should not be paying income tax at all,' says my colleague Dr Madsen Pirie in his 2009 Adam Smith Institute book *Zero Base Policy*. 'Those on low incomes find it hard enough to make ends meet as it is, without the additional burden of income tax.'

Madsen recommends that the starting level for income tax should therefore be set above the minimum wage — at least £12,000 a year. That would take seven million low-paid workers out of tax entirely, transforming their lives. He calculates that it would be the equivalent of a 14% pay rise for the average worker. And that means that millions who currently depend on benefits and tax credits would be lifted out of dependency and become self-supporting.

Any Treasury officials who are reading this will by now have had to pour themselves a stiff malt and delve into Chapman's *Homer* to recover their peace of mind. Because the Treasury's disgustingly dirty secret is that the poor pay most tax. Indeed, if the Treasury stopped taxing anyone below the minimum wage, it would lose around £19 billion in revenues, which is a fair chunk of change. So it all comes back to saving money and cutting spending. Still, the TaxPayers Alliance has estimated that there is an easy £100 billion of waste in government spending, so there is plenty of hope there; and they figure the cost of quangos to the taxpayer has risen by £41 billion a year. So for just six months' worth of additional quango spending, we could indeed take everyone on the minimum wage out of tax entirely. Strikes me as a no-brainer.

The fortune account

Let me park one other idea that has been on my mind for some time. Since 1995, in fact, when Madsen Pirie and I published an Adam Smith Institute report called *The Fortune Account*. It is a simple enough idea. At present our state benefits and indeed our state pension system works as a kind of chain letter. You pay money as taxes to the Treasury today, and some other person, today or tomorrow, draws that cash from the Treasury as benefits or pensions. Our fortune account, by contrast, gives them a sort of knapsack that they carry through life, paying in when they can and drawing out when they need to.

Not only does that safeguard fortune account holders — everyone, in other words — against whatever life throws for them, it will leave them better off. In the first place, they will be more careful what they draw out, because they will see it as their money, not someone else's (or — a recipe for real profligacy — the government's). And they will be more inclined to throw in a bit extra when they are feeling flush, which not many people do with taxes.

Private insurers and savings institutions can run fortune accounts, so politicians will be kept away from messing around with them for political reasons and dipping into people's cash for their own political purposes. It would offer people a real alternative to relying on state welfare, and would rebuild the UK's savings pool, so badly eroded in the last decade or so of boom and bust. In 1995 it got many favourable comments, but it was an idea ahead of its time. But now…?

Pensions

While we are reforming welfare and setting up fortune accounts, we certainly need to do something with the state pension at the same time. It is perhaps the world's largest Ponzi scheme. Named after Charles Ponzi who invented pyramid schemes in 1920s Boston, the idea is that you get punters to pay in to your fund, promising them huge investment returns. (Ponzi promised to give his investors a 50% return in just three months, which should have sent them running, but in fact had them queuing up to hand over their cash.) Then you spend the money on champagne, gambling, fast cars, prostitutes, politicians and other unsavoury characters. Soon your customers ask for their money back, plus their promised returns, but by this time, since the deal you are offering looks so spectacular, even more punters have also given you their money, so you use half of it to pay off the first lot and use the rest on champagne, gambling and all the other stuff. And so it goes on, until one day you cannot quite pull in enough new investors and the pyramid collapses, whereupon you go to jail, where there is no champagne, gambling or fast cars, but at least there will be plenty of prostitutes and politicians to talk to.

The politicians who run our state pension scheme should certainly be in jail for running a Ponzi scheme, since they have been doing it since Lloyd George promised people 'ninepence for fourpence' which of course looked an even more eye-popping deal than Ponzi ever dared to suggest. We pay in today for our old age, but the money we pay is not saved or invested — it goes straight out again as pension benefits to current pensioners. We all just have to hope that the next generation will be even bigger mugs than we are.

Hugely costly regulation, not to mention some

spectacular stealth taxes, have killed off more than half of the private pensions that people used to have through their workplaces, so unless you are a civil servant and have one of those coveted gold-plated pensions, you really are stuffed. Not that anyone these days can understand pensions anyway. There are some 35 different kinds of pension regulation all in effect in the UK, and it takes a two-year course to become a pension adviser. If you want to spend £20 on the national lottery, it is no questions asked, but if you want to save £20 for your retirement, you first need to find one of these highly-trained (and therefore very expensive) advisers, who (under the regulations) will speak Greek at you for two hours and ask you to fill in a twelve-page form that is written in a language that may once have been English. It is not surprising that so few people bother. Plainly, we need to slash the tax and the regulation and make group and individual pension saving schemes viable again, so people can look to their own resources in retirement, rather than having to rely wholly on the state and on politicians who are more interested in the next election than on the public's long term future.

Because the state pension has never provided a pension which MPs could justify as being adequate, Gordon Brown introduced the pension credit, to make sure that every pensioner got a decent amount to live on, even if they had no savings in addition to their state pension income. Unfortunately this benefit is means tested — that is, the more you have saved for yourself, the less of it you get. Derek Scott, the businessman and No 10 economics adviser whom Tony Blair put on Gordon Brown control, told me that Gordon really did think this extra benefit support would encourage people to save for their retirement, but of course it does the opposite. Most of the population, in fact, would be plain crazy to save for their retirement, because they would simply lose benefits as a result.

Meanwhile, with people living longer, working lives shorter, and a larger proportion of the population not paying in because they are in college or are unemployed, the state pension Ponzi scheme looks sicker and sicker. We really do need to bring its finances back into balance. Luckily the prominent actuary Alan Pickering has told us how in the 2004 Adam Smith Institute paper wittily entitled *How The Government Can Get Us Saving Again*.

Getting out of the state Ponzi scheme
Pickering recommends that we raise the state pension to around 40% of the average wage. That takes every pensioner above the current level of pension credit and abolishes the scourge of poverty in old age. Again, the Treasury folk have already looked away and started to pour themselves a large Glenlivet, but there is more. To pay for it you put up the state pension age to 68, and you keep indexing it to keep pace with the nation's rising life expectancy. Raising the pension age, in fact, liberates a surprising amount of money — enough to get the system back on an even financial keel.

Ideally, though, we want to get politicians out of pensions entirely. Hardly anyone trusts them to deliver people a decent state pension after their forty years or so of hard work. Indeed, a MORI survey that pollster Sir Bob Worcester did for the Adam Smith Institute some years ago revealed that more people thought they might have an affair with a member of the royal family than thought they would ever get a decent state pension.

Again, Sweden can teach us how to do it, though the idea

is not original nor unique to them. Many countries have in fact replaced state Ponzi-scheme pensions with proper, individuated pension accounts. Sweden's system was in such a mess that the government appointed a panel of wise experts to tell them how to fix it. After taking evidence and deliberating for a year, the panel told them bluntly that the Ponzi system was unfixable and that Sweden needed to move its pension to a proper savings basis.

About a dozen or more countries now do the same, and again the idea is simple. Instead of handing over money to the Treasury, which they immediately pay out again to other people, you hand the same money over to a private savings fund of your choice — there may be a dozen or a score of them — and they invest it. Over the years, that grows into a nice big pension. Your contributions can be collected by the funds privately, or perhaps more efficiently, by HM Customs & Revenue along with your taxes — but they hand it straight out again to your chosen fund. In Sweden, if you do not nominate a particular savings fund, the government will choose one for you: and they usually choose ones that are rather conservatively managed, which of course has been exactly the right place to be over the last couple of years. It rather makes sense: which is why so many countries are doing something similar. It is well past time for us to fall in with them.

9

CRIME AND JUSTICE

Crime, particularly local crime, vandalism and anti-social behaviour, always scores high on the opinion polls of public concerns. And so it should. About 10 million crimes of one sort or another are recorded each year in England and Wales. About a quarter of it is vandalism, and a fifth is criminal damage to property. There are around 1.5 million car thefts or thefts from cars. Around one in 40 homes are burgled each year, roughly 900,000 cases, and there are roughly 3 million fraudulent credit-card transactions. Even more worrying, there are about 2 million crimes of violence — over half of them muggings and other violence against strangers.

In financial terms, nobody has the foggiest idea how much crime costs us, but everyone agrees that it is a lot. The Home Office back in 2000 reckoned that crime cost us about £80 billion a year in today's money, equivalent to £3,000 per household or another 20p on the standard rate of income tax. A survey by the British Chambers of Commerce suggested that crime cost businesses alone some £12.6 billion in 2008, up a fifth on 2003.

The soaring number of recorded violent crimes, and the fact that weapons are used in about a fifth of them, may be one reason why people believe that crime is getting worse. Three out of four of us believe that crime has increased nationally, and just over a third of us reckon that it has gone up locally too. Even more of us think that knife and gun crime has been rising nationally and locally.

Indeed, the UK's crime record is one of Europe's (and the developed world's) worst. It has a higher murder rate than most of our near EU neighbours, the fifth highest robbery rate in the EU, and the fourth worst record on burglaries, with double the number of offences recorded in Germany and France. Our violent crime statistics are comfortably ahead of nearly all other countries, twice the level of Belgium or Sweden and four times that of France or (perhaps surprisingly) the United States.

Our dysfunctional justice system

All this could explain why we have one of the world's largest prison populations, and why our prisons are still bursting at the seams. Yet it could be a lot higher if every violent crime was properly prosecuted. The Criminal Prosecutions Service (CPS) is under the same target pressures as every other quango, and its success targets lead it to prosecute cases with the best chance of success. Arguably it is right to concentrate public money on prosecutions that are more like to succeed, but the targets mean that easy but small cases are often prosecuted while difficult but major incidents are not.

When cases do get to court, it is another predictable bureaucratic mess. The time of everyone involved is badly managed, and since lawyers are generally paid by the hour, everyone has an incentive to string the proceedings out. Expensively paid judges may sit for as little as 26 days a year. The courts' IT system is hopeless, and is only being upgraded because nobody can get spare parts for the old one. The new system for magistrates' courts turned into a fifteen-year fiasco, as is common with government IT schemes. Files get lost or go astray in transit between police and prosecutors, causing delays, postponements and a lot of wasted time, inconvenience for witnesses and even higher bills from the lawyers.

If by chance this appallingly hopeless system does produce a prosecution, it is unlikely to have much effect, except in terms of costing the public money. Young offenders flaunt their electronic tags as a mark of toughness. Two-thirds of them are reconvicted within two years. Meanwhile, two-fifths of people who are given fines or community sentences are reconvicted in that same time. More shockingly still, three-quarters of those sent to prison for six months or less will be back within the same period. Even longer sentences do not seem to present any discouragement: a quarter of those jailed for over four years will be back before too long. That is despite the fact that the prison authorities have their charges' complete attention 24 hours a day, in which you might think they could teach them a bit about how to be better and more law-abiding citizens. But when they are given scant rehabilitation therapy or education in jail, and are tossed out with no job and just a few quid in their pocket, what do we expect of them?

Abuse of legislative power

Despite this sorry record, policy over the last ten or fifteen years has focused entirely on looking tough and spending more on enforcement. Government spending on the criminal justice system has risen by a third since 1997 to around £25 billion a year today. The bulk of that has gone to provide bigger budgets for the police, the courts and the prisons, despite the fact that all of these institutions are clearly dysfunctional. Not more cash, but only a radical and complete reform of all of them is likely to have any impact on crime in the UK. Meanwhile, hardly any attention has been given to crime prevention, despite numerous studies showing how important it is to take action early when things start to go wrong in the lives of young people in particular. Despite all Tony Blair's talk of being tough on the *causes* of crime, our politicians have instead sought to look tough on crime itself. That, after all, is much easier and plays better in the tabloids.

The political imperative to look tough has led to an avalanche of new laws that basically allow any of us to be treated like criminals, allowing the police to ratchet up the number of supposed offences that are out there, and of course the number that they apprehend. When the Terrorism Act 2000 was going through Parliament, everyone thought they knew what its purpose was — stopping people who might want to blow us up, basically. But its scope was made so broad that perfectly innocent people have been caught up by it too. Under it, Sally Cameron was arrested (two squad cars, sirens blaring) for *walking* along a cycle path near the harbour in Dundee; while octogenarian Labour activist Walter Wolfgang was apprehended for daring to heckle Jack Straw at the 2005 Labour conference.

The Terrorism Act allowed the government to nominate specific places where the police could use stop-and-search powers. MPs might have thought that this authority would be limited to stopping potential terrorists who were looking shifty outside nuclear power stations or army barracks. No: ministers swiftly declared the whole of London as a stop-and-search area. They do not need any cause to stop you, but if you whip out your Leica to take a tourist photo under the eye of one of London's million-odd CCTV cameras, you are probably asking for it. In 2009 an entire film crew were stopped while interviewing me outside their office, and made to fill in the standard yellow 'Macpherson' forms with their name, address, race, sex and even height and weight.

Likewise, the Serious Organised Crime and Police Act 2005 was billed as a measure to make the mafia quake in their boots. But it allowed police to arrest lone protestor Steve Jago near Downing Street and confiscate copies of the *Vanity Fair* article on Tony Blair he was handing out as 'politically motivated material'; and before long the vegan chef Maya Evans was arrested for the 'crime' of standing at the Cenotaph in Whitehall and simply reading out the names of soldiers killed in Iraq.

It gets worse, though. Under the Anti-Social Behaviour Order (ASBO) system, you can wind up in jail without even going to court. The local council serves an ASBO on you for whatever they deem fit — using the word 'gross', not tidying your garden, sarcasm, laughing at your neighbours, giving people a slow handclap or letting your budgie sing too loud, just to cite some recent cases. Break the order, and you go to jail. You go directly to jail. You do not pass go. You do, however, collect a criminal record.

Parliament never intended people to go to jail because the next-door neighbour takes exception to their budgie. There should be some sanction against our police and other authorities who use the laws in ways that are far removed from what Parliament intended when it was debating them.

Until ministers finally yielded to the public's outrage and reined them in, for example, local authorities were launching about 1,000 covert surveillance operations a month under anti-terrorist laws. Why? So they could monitor people who were not recycling rubbish, or dropping litter, or fly tipping, or parking in the wrong place, or letting their dogs foul the footpath. Croydon council even used surveillance powers to keep an eye on someone trimming his hedge. It is not enough that people who are subject to such bullying can go to court and try to prove their innocence — not even that did Jago and Evans much good, since they ended up with criminal records.

Where police and officials usurp the powers that Parliament has given them, they should be punished. And frankly, when government ministers and whips push laws through our poodle Parliament without understanding how they might devastate people's lives, they should be taken out and horsewhipped, too. In Denmark, for example, a new law to prevent knife crime has put more than fifty people in jail because they had a knife on them or a knife in their car. In most cases, the defendants had been craftsmen leaving their tools in the car after work, anglers coming home from a fishing trip, or just people carrying a multitool in case of a breakdown. The overwhelming majority of those put in prison under this law are peaceful people who present no threat to anyone else.

You might think it could not happen here. Think again. Paul Clarke, a former soldier, found a sawn-off shotgun and handed it into the police. He was immediately charged of possessing a weapon, and prosecuted. The jury found him guilty after the judge pointed out that anyone in possession of a gun, even if like him they had rung the police station to say they were bringing it in, would face the same sentence (five years in jail). Maybe Paul Clarke acted foolishly in touching the gun at all, or maybe he thought it better to get it into safe hands as soon as possible, rather than leave it lying about. It does not matter. According to the law, he is just as bad as an armed gangster. And the alarming thing is that it could happen to any of us.

Now I come to think of it, horsewhipping is too good for them.

Getting the police to engage

Prevention is better than cure, particularly if the cure is as heavy-handed as so much recent legislation has been. Of course, it is *local* crime which most affects and concerns people, and in the fight against that, they would like to have the police as partners. Yet as Jill Kirby, the energetic head of the Centre for Policy Studies put it to me, people too often feel as if the police are on the side of the state rather than on the side of the citizen.

In *The Plan*, Douglas Carswell and Dan Hannan make the point that all the Macpherson paperwork is counterproductive. It does huge damage to the relationship between the police and the public. We *want* our community police to be able to engage with the public, and question what people are up to, without making a big thing of it and having to spend five minutes filling out a form every time they do. Nobody minds a reasonable question about what they are up to, with an innocent answer quickly accepted. It is the officious paperwork — and the thought that, though you were going about your own business perfectly innocently, your personal details are going to be stored in and pored over by some police computer — that turns a trivial enquiry into an 'us and them' confrontation. What we really want is to feel that the police are with us and concerned for us, not that they regard as all as criminals.

This is a particular problem in the case of young people.

Early and positive intervention with young people is the best way to prevent them offending in the future. Yet while a friendly word from a police officer might encourage a young person to behave more responsibly, confronting them with a pad of official forms is more likely to alienate them and feed their resentment. There are 100,000 young people entering the criminal justice system every year, with official warnings, reprimands or convictions. The figure cannot be helped by the fact that bad laws and police bureaucracy have turned the relationship between police and the community adversarial.

Apart from scrapping the paperwork, there are of course other minor things that can be done to bring the police closer to the public. Why do police stations have to be the most forbidding looking buildings, for example? Do all police officers have to be based in a police station at all? With modern technology, it is easy to keep spread out, be on the move, and yet keep in touch.

A simple but effective way of forcing the police to engage with the public has been made by John Blundell, the towering networker who stood down as Director General of the Institute of Economic Affairs at the end of 2009, after seventeen years of running the granddaddy of the Westminster think-tanks. Taking an idea from the reforming New York police chief Bill Bratton, he says that police stations should simply close their in-house canteens, forcing police officers to get their lunch and their warming coffee and donuts in local cafes. Yes, it would mean giving them an allowance – we do not want local cafe owners thinking they have to give officers a freebie to stay on their right side. But the point is that it would get officers out of the station and into the very heart of the local community, where they would be very visible. In the informal atmosphere of a local cafe, they would also seem more human – and more approachable too, which today they are not.

At present, police patrol in twos. It is partly something that goes back to Magna Carta, which says that people cannot be convicted on the word of a single officer of the state, but it is also about police forces fearing themselves liable if a lone officer runs into difficulties. The trouble is that two police officers walking round together are much more likely to talk to each other than to say hello to passing members of the public. People are more likely to tell a single officer of their suspicions about something than they are if there are two: again, an encounter with a single officer feels more personal, an encounter with two feels more official. And of course, officers in pairs can be only in half the number of places as can those patrolling individually, so the police are not seen as much and have only half the presence they might otherwise.

Of course, it all needs to be done with a modicum of competence, although that is often rather hard to find in the UK police and criminal justice system. In the Netherlands, the police carry PDAs — 'personal digital assistants' like iPhones, which give them a map showing where every other officer is. That means they can put themselves around widely, and engage with the public, as individuals; but they can get support quickly and whenever they need it. Copying this idea, Jan Berry, the police 'red tape tsar' (can you believe that?) issued 27,000 of them to our own bluebottles. It had, of course, absolutely no impact on the scant amount of time constables spend on the beat, or the vast amount of time they spend recording incidents. Frankly, we would be better contracting our entire police force out to the Dutch.

Making the police accountable

There is a wider social dimension to crime, of course. There is a benefits system that breaks up families and leaves children, particularly boys, with no adult male role model. There is a drug culture that leads to neglect of children, which adds to the problem of young people growing up without being properly socialised. There is the growth in officialdom that makes people feel less willing to intervene when they see something wrong happening. There is a state education system that cares more about passing exams than turning out upright citizens.

The police cannot be expected to cure all these ills. Yet the rift between the police and communities makes them worse. Some years ago the Adam Smith Institute polled both the public and police officers, asking them what they thought were the most important local crime issues. The answers hardly overlapped at all.

Carswell and Hannan reckon this is because police authorities simply do not represent the public. Police chiefs take their cue from the Home Office — with its central funding streams, targets, audit and inspections — rather than from the rather toothless local bodies. In any case, the police authorities are not democratic but appointed bodies — quangos of local worthies including councillors, magistrates and Home Office representatives — so they feel no moral mandate to question how their local police force is working.

They should be scrapped, say Carswell and Hannan, and replaced by directly elected Sheriffs, rather like those in the United States. The Sheriffs would appoint and dismiss police chiefs, and would set out the targets and policing plans for the local force. They, and not the CPS, would be in charge of prosecutions. They would be in charge of the local probation system too. This, believe Carswell and Hannan, would improve accountability and more closely reflect and serve local feelings about crime and justice.

I am not completely sold on this idea, though it might well be better than the present arrangement in which all the power resides in chief constables and the Home Office, and in which the public themselves have no effective say. Unless candidates for Sheriff were very well known locally, however — and high-profile, attention-seeking candidates are not necessarily who you want to run your police and prosecutions system — the election would probably boil down to yet another contest between the political parties. And local politicians are not necessarily the people we want to run the justice system either. Still, it is worth a try.

We should think even more radically. Contracting out has brought benefits in just about every other area of local service provision. Evidence not just from the UK but from around the world indicates that merely suggesting that services such as refuse collection should be contracted out to private bidders saves local taxpayers around 20%, while actually going to tender saves up to 40%, and – if done properly – produces a more flexible service. Why do we imagine that the provision of local police and community support services cannot be done, better and more cheaply, by competitive providers? This too is worth a try. We should give local police chiefs – or Sheriffs if that is what we end up with – the power to tender out whatever parts of the local policing job they think could benefit from it. My guess is that they would discover that they could provide the community with more, and more engaged, front line policing, at lower cost to the local taxpayers."

Crime prevention

There is a familiar pattern. It may start with bad parenting; then the kids, uncontrolled, causing trouble on the street: petty crime and drugs; then it is too late. When I sat as a school governor and we had to exclude a pupil for appalling, threatening or violent behaviour, my colleagues used to say despairingly that we might as well book their future prison accommodation while we were at it. Why does our justice system find it so impossible to take action early, when it is needed?

There is a wealth of international evidence on how to identify and tackle the risk factors that draw young people into a life of criminality. Indeed, the Home Office spent £250 million in 1999 creating a so-called crime reduction strategy on the basis of it. But, as Max Chambers, Ben Ullmann and Irvin Waller say in their 2009 Policy Exchange report *Less Crime, Lower Costs*, the whole programme (as happens so often) was mired in central targets, management and financial control, when in fact the focus should have been local. After just a few years, the money was cut off and the whole thing dropped.

The spin doctors, at least, were undaunted, and with equal fanfare the National Crime Reduction Board was set up in 2007. Not that it has any budget; nor do the justice and children's ministers bother to turn up at its meeting; and it seems unable to construct any coordinated approach to early and effective intervention. Spending on crime prevention remains *ad hoc*, and is tiny compared with what is spent on dealing with crime once it occurs — just 5% of the Youth Justice Board's (YJB) budget, compared with 75% spent on custody. Local authorities, meanwhile, are perfectly happy to see kids locked up on the YJB's budget, rather than pay for the police and intervention programmes that might prevent it.

Such a funding system is perverse, of course. The National Audit Office (NAO) estimates that preventing just one in ten young offenders from ending up in custody would save £100 million a year; a successful prevention programme could produce enormous benefits for the taxpayer. Yet crime prevention does not have to be expensive. According to the report, some American crime-prevention programmes claim benefits of 25 times what they spend.

You cannot expect people to spend money, however, if the costs appear on their budget and the benefits show on somebody else's. Certainly, it would be possible to take bits of the police or Sure Start budgets and put them towards early intervention. A more durable solution might be something like the tax increment funding idea, with the local authorities raising a bond for crime prevention, and the benefits in terms of future prosecution and custody budgets being earmarked to help pay it off.

The one-sided war on drugs
The Home Office estimated that four-fifths of crime is drug related. It is not just the turf wars and gang violence, nor even the dealing itself. There are the thefts and robberies by which users finance their supplies. Nearly all of it is down to problem users with generally chaotic lives and a heroin or crack cocaine habit. Recreational users are responsible for hardly any crime at all — except, of course, their use of recreational drugs.

The financial cost is equally alarming. The Department of Health estimates the economic and social cost of Class A drug use at around £15 billion a year, or maybe £45,000 per user (though because of the illicit nature of the thing, nobody knows exactly how many problem users there are).

Naturally, the politicians of most parties have chosen to display their concern at all this by adopting 'get tough' policies. Drugs, even the nation's second-favourite recreational drug, cannabis, have been kicked up the penalty ladder. The tabloids love it, but all it does is to raise the risks for dealers, who then charge higher prices to users and send even greater profits back to producers, who reckon they are on to a good business and produce even more. Roughly 90% of the price of street drugs is actually the illegality premium, rather than the cost of producing the stuff itself.

The struggle has raged for decades, but now the war on drugs, as they say, is over. Drugs won. Today in England and Wales there are about 500,000 regular ecstasy users, another 750,000 or more using cocaine, and something over 2.5 million users of cannabis; and most of them are pretty content about it all.

Freedom as the best prescription
Some countries, like the Netherlands, have allowed limited legal access to drugs, but in 2001 Portugal became the only EU country to decriminalise all drugs. Interestingly, none of the nightmare scenarios painted by opponents — from rampant increases in drug use among the young to Lisbon becoming a haven for 'drug tourists' actually happened. Perhaps, as in the UK, there were so many people using drugs to begin with that the market was already satisfied.

The spectacular rise in heroin addition in the UK correlates very well with our attempts to suppress it. From 1926 and for the next forty years, the policy used to be that dealers would be prosecuted, but doctors could prescribe heroin to registered addicts in order to spare them the distress of withdrawal. It worked well until about 1960, when the numbers of addicts started to rise, and illicit sale of the drug by doctors did for it. From the mid 1960s, only specialised clinics were allowed to prescribe, then in the 1970s, we moved to giving addicts the supposedly less harmful methadone instead. Methadone is cheap, which is why the authorities prefer it over costly rehabilitation programmes; but most users and plenty of doctors reckon methadone to be much worse than heroin, and of course it does not help them out of their chaotic lives.

Things might be changing, though. In the four-year Randomised Injecting Opioid Treatment Trial (RIOTT) in London, Brighton and Darlington, heroin users were given free access to drugs in supervised, clinical conditions. The scheme led to significant reductions in the crimes committed, and the street drugs taken, by users, particularly when they were given heroin rather than methadone. And of course treating heroin addiction as a medical condition like alcoholism, rather than a criminal tendency, allows addicts to volunteer for rehabilitation programmes, which is ultimately what the great majority of them want.

In *Zero Base Policy*, Madsen Pirie sums it up like this. The policy with the best chance of success, he says, would be to medicalise hard drugs as in the RIOTT trials, and legalise the production, sale and use of recreational drugs such as ecstasy and cannabis. Their production, quality, sale and place of use would be controlled, just as they are for alcohol and tobacco; but it would no longer be illegal for adults to possess and use them.

Without the criminal risk involved in supplying drugs, their price would plummet (though the government would no doubt be quick to tax them). The worrying question is whether that, and the new, legal availability of drugs, would lead to many more people taking them up. Madsen thinks not. Tobacco, he says, is legal, but most people choose to remain (or become) non-smokers. They are well aware of the risks to their own health and the discomfort that smoking causes others. Indeed, governments make cigarettes carry stark health warnings, and they are likely to do exactly the same with legalised drugs. Binge drinking too is legal, and some people do it, but only a minority. It is unlikely to be any different with drugs.

In any event, if problems do emerge, at least they can be dealt with. Right now, the supply of illicit drugs is out of control, which exposes users to countless hazards, such as uncertain quality, contaminated supplies, and even their own ignorance about the safety and effects of what they take. As America decided when it voted to end alcohol prohibition — the most notable effect of which was the rise of Al Capone rather than much reduction in America's drinking — whatever the problems of legalisation, they cannot be any worse than what we have now.

Too many laws, not enough justice
I once went to an election meeting held by our local Monster Raving Loony Party candidate. As election meetings went, it was more attractive than most, being held in a pub. The candidate came in — he was wearing a rather fetching green polka-dot cotton dress — and announced that he had only two policies, but they focused directly on the main things that worried people. On the economy, he said that he intended to shorten the unemployment lines by asking people to stand closer together. On crime, he said he would cut crime by reducing the number of laws. I thought these were both

eminently deliverable election promises.

Out of the mouth of babes and sucklings, not to mention Monster Raving Loony Party candidates. We certainly *do* have too many laws that make criminals out of perfectly innocent people like Sally Cameron, Walter Wolfgang, Steve Jago, Maya Evans and, if we are not careful, you and me. The question is what to do about it.

In 2009 the Conservatives said that all it would take is to push one single, consolidated 'repeal' bill through Parliament, amending all the measures of the last dozen years that have done so much to erode our liberties and create the unhealthy 'us and them' adversarial relationship between the police and the public. Frankly, I do not believe that such an approach is practicable. A free society does indeed need strong powers to protect its citizens against terrorism by those who resent its freedoms and would gladly overthrow them. Our children need to be safeguarded against those who would harm them. We need to protect our values and institutions from those who would tear them down without regret. The problem is to do all that, without letting politicians, officials and police officers treat us all as if we were terrorists, drug pushers, paedophiles or subversives. Plainly, this is going to need a bit of thought, not just one hasty piece of legislation.

Giving the Devil — and ourselves — the benefit of law
In Robert Bolt's 1954 play *A Man For All Seasons*, about the strife between Henry VIII and Sir Thomas More, there is a revealing dialogue between More and his son-in-law William Roper. It goes like this:

Roper: 'So now you'd give the Devil the benefit of law!'
More: Yes. What would you do? Cut a great road through the

law to get to the Devil?'

Roper: 'I'd cut down every law in England to do that!'

More: 'Oh? And when the last law was down, and the Devil turned round on you — where would you hide, Roper, the laws all being flat? This country's planted thick with laws from coast to coast — man's laws, not God's — and if you cut them down — and you're just the man to do it — do you really think you could stand upright in the winds that would blow then? Yes, I'd give the Devil benefit of law, for my own safety's sake.'

This country has a proud history of protecting its citizens against the devil of arbitrary and over-mighty government, stretching back to Magna Carta in 1215, and indeed beyond. Most of these limits on government were fought over bitterly, and while many were not even written down in law, they came to be accepted as the base and fabric of our liberal society. In recent years this base and fabric has been almost systematically undermined — and all in the name of protecting our interests. Indeed, many people have cheered as our liberties have been sapped. But we need that fabric of freedom to protect ourselves, not just against hostile outsiders, but against the corruption of power at home too.

Take the principle of *habeas corpus*, the right not to be detained without trial, which goes back to Anglo-Saxon times. It has gone. The Anti-Terrorism, Crime And Security Act 2001 allowed the authorities to detain people whom they thought were terrorists, but were unwilling to prosecute. Well, terrorists are bad people, so you might not worry — until you know that it takes only the word of a single judge to decide whether or not you are a suspect. That is not much protection for innocent people like you and me.

Trial by jury is another principle going back to Magna

Carta. It is a vital limit on the abuse of justice by those in power because juries are independent. It has gone. The Criminal Justice Act 2003 says that cases can be tried by judges without juries if they are likely to be long or complicated. And who decides which cases might be long and complicated? Not a jury, you can be sure of that.

The point about rights is that they protect us in the long run, even though they might have unwelcome effects from time to time. *Double jeopardy* dates back to the twelfth century, and is designed to prevent the authorities from re-trying their enemies over and over again for the same offence, in the hope of wearing them down or even eventually getting a guilty verdict. Yet the Criminal Justice Act 2003 overturned this 800-year-old right in cases where 'new and compelling evidence' arises. And who decides what is 'new and compelling'? You guessed.

The right to remain silent has gone too. Juries (if you are lucky enough to get one) can be instructed to regard your silence as something fishy. You might prefer to say nothing to the police because you figure they will gladly mangle your words in order to meet their conviction targets, but now it counts against you. In some fraud cases the *presumption of innocence* has gone too: you have to convince the Revenue and Customs that you *were not* on the fiddle.

Another strong principle of civil liberties is our right to *privacy* — to go about our lawful business without being constantly snooped on by the authorities. That has gone too. Not only is there the National Identity Database and ID cards; but the Regulation of Investigatory Powers Act 2000 compelled UK internet service providers to monitor our email and web browsing habits and hand the information on to the authorities whenever they demand it — without us users knowing anything about it. When the law was debated, only nine state agencies were authorised in this way. Now, with no debate and just ministerial say-so, there are 792 of them (including 474 local councils) who can demand our data. And they say we are living in a democracy.

We are all — potentially — guilty

Only the guilty have anything to fear, they say; but then with laws that make *anything* an arrestable offence, we are all potentially guilty. When one stray comment in an email can send you to the slammer, our fingers should be trembling on the mouse, because *freedom of speech* is near death too.

For example, grandmother Pauline Howe wrote to her local council to say she considered a gay rights march they had sanctioned was a 'public display of indecency'. She was promptly visited by two constables and told she might have committed a 'hate crime'. Pretty intimidating, I would think. Next, family campaigner Lynette Burrows faced a police investigation after saying on radio that she did not think that homosexuals should be allowed to adopt. Again, whatever you think of her beliefs, should she not be allowed to express them? Meanwhile, well-known TV and stage comedians complained that new 'race hate' laws would stop them telling the traditional jokes about Irish, Polish, and Jewish stereotypes. The government assured them there was no chance of it: but if you noticed, they have stopped all the same.

On top of all this there have been innumerable cases of people being arrested, and getting criminal records, for wearing T-shirts with politically incorrect or 'offensive' messages like 'Bollocks to Blair' or suggesting that the Iraq war is criminal. You can be spot fined by the police and 1,406 other officials, from litter wardens to dog-catchers, for something as minor as dropping an apple core; and if you contest it, you will be taken to court and possibly fined a four-figure sum.

The laws and official bullying that limits free speech in the UK are a disaster. It is essential that people should be able to say what they like, even if it is sometimes offensive to others. One of the reasons why science and endeavour moved from renaissance Italy to liberal Britain was that the forces of religion persecuted the likes of Copernicus and Galileo, whose ideas offended their doctrine. We develop through debate, even heated debate. But now, here, the forces of political correctness are persecuting those who offend their doctrine too.

Many people find holocaust denial offensive, for example; but that should not make it illegal. It *is* of course — a few years ago an Australian teacher who made comments about the holocaust in the UK faced a European Arrest Warrant for extradition to be prosecuted in Austria (where holocaust denial is illegal, unlike in either Australia or the UK). On BBC *Question Time* in November 2009, the Justice Secretary Jack Straw assured the British National Party leader Nick Griffin that there was nothing to stop him making revisionist comments about the holocaust in the UK. But that is a straight lie from a politician. Nobody should sensibly entrust their liberty to that. If you can be whisked out to an Austrian jail for something you say in the UK, that kills free speech here too, I would say.

People hurt each other's feelings all the time, but that it is something that we all have to deal with: it is not something for the law to get involved in. All the time when I lived in Washington DC, I got called 'honkey' by the blacks and 'limey' by the whites. I did not like it much, but I got on with life. If, however, someone had put their face into mine and told me 'I'm going to kill you, you honkey/limey bastard!' — well, then I might have gone to the police.

Systematic replacement of civil liberties

So you can see why I do not think some quick repeal measure will amount to much against this unyielding erosion of our rights and liberties by those with the whip hand of political and official power. We need instead to rediscover the reasons why these rights and liberties emerged in the first place, and to begin to understand once more why they are vital to us in the long term, even if they get in our way from time to time. The whole point of them is that they *should* get in the way of those in power who think they know better how to run our lives than we do ourselves.

My colleague Madsen Pirie has suggested that we need a year-long enquiry into the rights of the citizen and the limits to government power over us. It would have to be chaired by senior and respected judges who understood the purpose of the law and the principles of rights and justice. It would take evidence from citizens who felt their freedoms had been threatened by arbitrary and bullying officials and intrusive laws. It would investigate how to ensure that laws were used only for the purposes that Parliament intended, and not to make criminals of us all. Its deliberations would raise the national debate, alert people to the threat of unrestrained centralised power, and find a consensus about the boundary between our private lives and the public interest. And with any luck, it would come up with recommendations and measures to restore and entrench our civil liberties and protect us from politicians who really think they are trying to help us, even as they abuse us with their arbitrary and oppressive power.

10

THE BULLY STATE

AN END TO NANNY PLAYS HARDBALL

What killjoys. In 2009 the new Islington store of fashion chain Joy launched an enterprising promotion, in which the first 25 customers to turn up in their underwear would get free outfits. Rather a fun idea, you might think.

But the long arm of the law did not think it so amusing. (There is a lot of truth in the old joke: Q — 'How many police constables does it take to screw in a light bulb?' A — 'I wouldn't make jokes if I were you, sir, this is a very serious matter.') No sooner were the 25 lucky ladies assembled outside in their smalls than the bluebottles (in the now-standard hi-vis jackets and body armour) turned up and accused them all of committing public indecency. That, of course, is an arrestable offence — actually, everything these days is an arrestable offence, as you will find if you drop an apple core or try to sell a squirrel. Faced with the prospect of being arrested, handcuffed and marched off to the nick, still in their undies, to be held, questioned, DNA-swabbed, fin-gerprinted, cautioned, charged and maybe taken to court, they all grumpily covered up, saying that our bobbies must have lost their sense of humour.

Bureaucrat economics

No, they have not. They are just doing their job — which is
the whole problem. Politicians, in their anxiety to show us
how they are stamping out anti-social behaviour, hate crime,
offensiveness and litter, have passed laws that give the fuzz
powers to arrest, handcuff, swab, fingerprint (and all the rest)
just about anyone for just about any reason that comes up
their hump.

Fine, perhaps, if the cops use common sense. But you
cannot expect that, for reasons of simple bureaucrat
economics. If they do *not* intervene and people complain that
they are offended, the Old Bill will get pilloried for not doing
their job and MPs and tabloids will give them some sharp
tongue. If they *do* intervene, the worst that happens — to
them, at least — is that people think they were a bit heavy-
handed. Better that, of course, than letting crime go unchal-
lenged. That is why, when we give a power to bureaucrats —
council officials, rozzers, quangocrats or whoever — we
should realise that they are going to use it. Not just when it is
appropriate, but all the time. It is just simple self-preserva-
tion.

That is why these powers should not exist in the first
place. Sure, the peelers need authority to protect us against
terrorism, or stop breaches of the peace. But unless we want
to face arrest for over-filling our wheelie bins, our politicians
need to be much more precise about what the law is there for
— rather than imagining that state officials will apply them
sensibly.

The bully state

Forget the nanny state, we are now living in the *Bully State*, according to the former MSP Brian Monteith in his 2009 book of that name. Small, round, avuncular, ever smiling and with an enormous delight in causing mischief, he entered Edinburgh's Heriot-Watt University thinking he was a leftie before he realised that he had been a libertarian all along. He decided to promote those ideas through a career in (Conservative) politics, though his colleagues in the Scottish Parliament did not always share his delight in mischief. Now he has made a new career as an energetic and skilful campaigner for the Free Society and other bodies that support the cause of personal freedom.

The bully state, he says, is even more malevolent than the nanny state. In the bully state, politicians and official coerce the public into compliance with their own views about how we should live. From health warnings on cigarettes through compulsory crash helmets for motorcyclists and then rear seat belts, we have now arrived at the situation where people can be fined for smoking in their own cars and Marmite can be banned in school sandwiches because it is 'too salty'.

'Today's politicians,' he tells me over a pint of heavy in a well-known Edinburgh watering hole, 'say we are mature enough to elect them into office, but not mature enough to decide for ourselves what we should eat, drink, smoke or drive. They have given officials draconian powers of entry and surveillance to terrorise householders into using the right rubbish bin and to force shopkeepers into hiding their cigarette stocks under the counter. In many places you cannot even have a glass of wine at an open-air picnic. And it is not just a left-wing thing — politicians of all colours seem to want to bully us into doing things their way.'

I suppose it is this sort of authoritarianism that made Islington Council seek the closure of a café serving

Caribbean food because its menu and its customers did not seem ethnically diverse enough to them. Or why home baking stalls have been banned at school fundraising events on the grounds that you cannot be sure that every parent's kitchen has the latest stainless steel food hygiene equipment. Or why Coventry stopped an Al Jolson tribute act from 'blacking up' as the singer did in the 1920, because it is 'racist'. No doubt they will be banning pantomime dames next, which means Sir Ian McKellen will be out of a job for sure.

It probably explains too, why the food and rural affairs department Defra in 2009 proposed banning 'buy one, get one free' (BOGOF) offers in supermarkets, on the grounds that it made people buy too much food, which was then wasted. And waste, of course, is bad. They ignored the fact that supermarkets use BOGOF to shift food that is near the end of its sell-by date, so without it the food would certainly be chucked anyway. Quite frankly, though, what damn business of some departmental official is it to decide the prices at which shops sell things?

Quite a lot, if you believe politicians — including the Conservatives, who ought to know better. I suppose if you wanted to be charitable you could blame it on the demands of the 24-hour news schedules rather than on the politicians' ignorance and stupidity, but the effect is the same. Whenever there is some problem like reports of binge drinking among young people, the nation's leaders jostle up to the microphones to tell the broadcasters (since nobody else is listening) how they are going to take 'immediate' and 'tough' action. Sadly, their 'tough' action is usually only tough on the symptoms, not the disease, and their 'immediate' action is usually a quarter-baked plan based on no evidence at all, which will be completely counterproductive and will cause immense damage for several years before it is finally abandoned and replaced with some other quarter-baked plan.

In the case of binge drinking, the plan is to put up the price of alcoholic drinks, particularly those that might appeal to young people. It will be a disaster, of course. When the Rudd government in Australia jacked up the price of pre-mixed drinks — such as alcopops — by 70%, consumption did indeed fall by 30%. Unfortunately, spirit sales jumped by 46% as the kids simply bought the rum and the syrupy drinks and mixed their own. And of course the kids poured themselves bigger measures than you got in the average alcopop bottle. The result was a 10% rise in alcohol consumption.

Australia also used to have the six-o'clock swill, as pub customers tanked up with as much as they could hold before the pubs closed in the early evening. I remember much the same in Scotland, when the pubs opened a few hours at lunchtime, then from 5pm to 10pm in the evening. They did not open at all on Sundays, though if you were a 'bona fide' traveller you could get a drink in a hotel. (Which prompted enterprising local bus companies to organise Sunday 'bona fide' trips taking parched Scots from one town to the next, and back again.) After Scotland deregulated in 1978, allowing 24-hour opening in some places, everything improved — there was less drunkenness, less violence, an easier job for the police who were no longer overstretched after 10.10pm (when 'drinking up time' officially ended) and a fall in alcohol-related illnesses. Pubs were no longer just male drinking holes, but started selling food and becoming much more like places you could take the family. However 'tough' our politicians want to appear in the media, we do not really want to go back to the old days.

Covering their back

Although Brian Monteith is right that the bully state has evil effects, I do not believe that it is always malevolent in intent. State nannying, and even state bullying, is I believe largely motivated by a desire to spare us from harm. That in turn might be motivated by the desire to avoid blame and litigation if we *do* come to harm, rather than any real human beneficence, but you cannot have everything. This is why, for example, East Bedfordshire parents were banned from coming to cheer their offspring at a school's sports day. After all, there could be paedophiles or kidnappers among those parents — how do you know, unless the Criminal Records Bureau (CRB) has vetted them all? Would you actually want to take the risk and put your job and reputation on the line?

The Working At Heights Regulations are of course designed to stop us being injured by using rickety stepladders or misusing ladders entirely. Unfortunately it means that churches now have to spend thousands of pounds on scaffolding to change a light bulb. Even Oxford's historic Bodleian Library has taken out its stepladders because of health and safety concerns. The only trouble is that students can no longer reach the books. Not that many of them can probably read anyway, given our school exams system.)

And private companies are getting embroiled in this sort of nonsense too. A drive-through McDonald's refused to serve a biker a hamburger on health and safety grounds, fearing he might try to eat it and ride at the same time. Tesco refused to sell cigarettes to a 59-year-old man with a Zimmer frame because he had no ID; two pensioners aged 68 and 70 were refused a bottle of wine for the same reason.

Competition between supermarkets is strong, though, and Asda topped its rival in the stupidity stakes by refusing to sell Chris Pether, 70, more than one lemon on the grounds that local youths had been known to throw such fruit at passers-by for a laugh.

Of course, if some budding athlete *was* kidnapped by a paedophile parent, or students *did* slip off the book ladder, or Mr Pether *did* throw his lemons at someone (or, perhaps, if under-age drinkers had been dressing up as pensioners and Zimmer-framing round the booze isles), then of course our newspapers would be down on our politicians like a ton of manure.

The only trouble is when the rules are followed slavishly rather than sensibly. The council in Birmingham told clowns in Zippo's circus that, in order to play trumpets in a three-minute comedy sketch, they needed to buy an expensive music licence — in each location they performed at (which is a lot). Your local Gilbert and Sullivan society also need to do the same before they can stage a summer operetta in a barn miles from anywhere, and they need an alcohol licence if they are to serve the punters a glass of wine at half time. These laws were of course designed to regulate and stop drunken raves in the middle of residential areas. Rules are supposed to exist to help us, not to enslave us.

Counterproductive nannying

Or damage us and expose us to even greater risk. After a school lollipop man was signed off on sick leave, father of three Craig Hodge volunteered to step in and help pupils at his kids' school cross a busy road to get to classes. Being a youth football coach he already had the CRB vetting, but Torbay council officials told him to quit and hang up his lollipop because he had not been properly trained. Maybe so, but is that not better than letting the kids cross on their own?

In December 2009 the government quickly reversed at least one small part of their vetting fascism, following total disbelief and outrage from millions of parents and other members of the general public. The plan that was *anyone* who comes into frequent contact with children should get a CRB check. On a rough calculation, it was reckoned that 11.3 million people, including parents who car-pooled their kids to school, would have to queue up for a sign-off from the police computer. The issue was highlighted when well-known authors like Quentin Blake and Terry Pratchett announced that they would no longer do school visits because they resented being treated like criminals. (It must be pretty hard to molest a child when you are speaking to a class of thirty of them plus the teacher; but that is the sort of absurd, overbearing rule that comes out of the bully state.)

Let us be grateful for small mercies. Now the quango in charge of making life hell for parents and running the world's largest child database — the so-called but not really Independent Safeguarding Authority — says it will not enforce the rules for the likes of Blake and Pratchett, though it will demand vetting for all those volunteer weekend football-coach parents. So what exactly is the law on this now? Not something passed by the people's representatives in Parliament, it seems, but something made up by ministers and officials to spare them embarrassment. It is no way to govern a country.

Apparently some 125,000 teenagers who work with fellow school kids as football coaches and the like will still have to get CRB checks too. It seems awful that the first thing we do when helpful young people reach the notional age of adulthood is to slap them with a demand to prove they are not paedophiles. At this rate, we will soon be vetting every kid in the sixth form, on the grounds that they spend their entire school day alongside younger ones and might molest or kidnap them. This whole system really does have to go.

One particularly shocking case of rules being taken to extremes was where ambulance crews were not allowed to help a nine-year-old girl who suffered a broken skull in a road accident because they were on their 30-minute lunch break and the rules say they must not be interrupted.

For my part, I have just ordered two cases of Nanny State Ale from the Brewdog Company in Aberdeenshire. At 1.1% it is no stronger than dishwater, of course, but Brewdog were getting so much flack for their stronger beers that they decided to give the health fascists a taste of their own tipple. Sometime soon I am going to invite my friends to a Nanny State Party, in which we will serve the stuff in recycled plastic cups, hand out five pieces of fruit and vegetables to everyone, and (under the gaze of CCTV cameras, of course), impose a strict 'No ID, No Entry' policy. I shall be inviting Jacqui Smith and Harriet Harman. You would be welcome: but do not expect me to show up, nor Quentin Blake and Terry Pratchett, for that matter. We might just nut someone.

From nannying to bullying
The greatest worries, though, begin when our leaders use their unrestrained political power to tell us how to live. Smoking, for example, might well do people harm, but it seems to me that if people want to accept the risk in order to enjoy the pleasure that smoking gives them, politicians have no right to stop them. They might have a right to inform

them, possibly, but not to stop them. Yet the pointy-headed metropolitan elite in Westminster see smoking as a rather vulgar, unpleasant habit born of weakness, and probably a bit working class too; so it has to be suppressed (or, since the tax revenues are a nice earner, at least driven underground). Even in our dilapidated democracy you cannot just stop people doing things you despise without some plausible excuse, so one has to be found. Ah yes: you cannot smoke in public places because the staff (waiters, bar staff and suchlike) would be forced to suffer your disease-laden second-hand smoke.

It might be, of course, that the staff might be smokers themselves, or are so delighted to have a job in the dismal economic climate that the politicians have bequeathed us, that they do not object at all. That, of course, does not stop the legislative puritans. It might be that all the members and staff of a club are content for folk to light up a cigar after dinner, but no, the legislators override their wishes in the name of purity. It might be pub customers would be happy with a separate smoking room, but no, that is not allowed either. It might be that air conditioning is so effective these days that the air inside is cleaner than the air on the street — but that all misses the point. The point is to impose a set of values, the values of our middle-class metropolitan politicians, on the rest of us.

Having saved us from smoking, the metro-prudes now plan to save us from sex. Prostitution is of course a rather old profession, but their aim is to stop it. Again, there has to be an excuse, and this time it is the supposed scourge of human trafficking.

Now where human beings are trafficked and forced into prostitution, I would be the first to condemn it. But in the

UK, at least, it is a minor problem that our parliamentary prudes have whipped up into a big one in order to justify their contempt for prostitution and to bully it out of existence. With much fanfare, they pointed to Operation Pentameter, which involved 55 police forces, six government departments and various non-government organisations, and led to the arrest of 528 sex traffickers. On the basis of that, Harriet Harman introduced a bill to make it illegal to pay for sex with a prostitute controlled by someone else. The problem is that the supposed evidence of 528 arrests is a total fraud. Ten of the 55 police forces arrested nobody at all. Some 122 of the 528 arrests that were claimed never actually happened (they were wrongly recorded, or phantom arrests designed to chase targets). Half (230) were women — suggesting that the Operation was yet another convenient excuse to harass prostitutes and clock up even more Brownie points for meeting arrest targets. Of the 406 real arrests, 153 had already been released weeks before the police announced their 'success', 106 without any charge at all, and 47 being cautioned for minor offences. Of the rest, 73 were charged with immigration breaches, 76 were on drugs raps, and others simply died or disappeared. Only 22 people were finally prosecuted for trafficking, including two women. Seven were acquitted. The net haul from this vast operation, in other words, was just 15 successful prosecutions. Of those, just five men were convicted of importing women and forcing them to work as prostitutes, two of whom were already in custody.

That is the 'huge success' on the basis of which Home Secretary Jacqui Smith (disgraced expenses fiddler with porn-watching husband employed at public expense) and then Harriet Harman (private-school educated and with aristocratic connections) claimed that 'thousands' of women were being trafficked. Sex workers, for their part, opposed the legislation. They know that every time governments 'get tough' on prostitution, they are the ones who suffer. As do their clients. If a lonely man, or one who has difficulty making long-term relationships, wants to pay for sex and a mature woman is willing to provide it, what right have any of the rest of us, whatever our moral objections, to outlaw it?

From bullying to judicial terrorism
Not only is personal freedom being eroded, the very rules of justice are being laid flat by executive power. The Proceeds of Crime Act 2000 was designed to 'hit criminals in the pocket' by allowing the authorities to seize assets that they had amassed as a result of their crimes. The quango that supervised this process cost more than the amount of swag recovered, of course, but you expect that sort of thing from Westminster.

Once a law has been debated, though, it is the easiest thing imaginable for the executive to extend it in ways that Parliament never intended. It just takes a statutory instrument, an order made by ministers and nodded through. Thanks to such a move by Home Secretary Alan Johnson in 2009, fare-dodgers and council tax shirkers now enjoy the same status as pimps and drug barons by being eligible to have their homes raided, their property seized and their financial assets frozen. It will not even be the police breaking down the door: power-drunk councils, quangos and public agencies such as Royal Mail have the same authority. This is not justice. It is judicial terrorism.

It gets worse (of course). The police want to be able to seize the assets even of those they *suspect* of criminal activity, even before any conviction has been made. At this rate, our justice system will soon look like America's — where prosecutors seize the assets of those they arrest on suspicion of crime, leaving them unable to finance their own defence against the charges. Neat, huh?

Nudge off

It is alarming that these are the same people who want to 'nudge' us into doing the 'right' thing. Nudging is the brainchild of Chicago Professor Richard Thaler, whom the Conservatives have hired to head their 'Star Chamber' inquisition on regulations. The idea is vey simple: kids are more likely to choose healthy food if you put that towards the front of the dinner counter and put the sticky puddings at the back; people are more likely to save into a workplace pension plan if they have to opt out of it rather than opt in to it; and there will be less splashes from gentlemen's urinals if you put a 'target' at the sweet spot. (Mr Armitage of sanitary ware makers Armitage Shanks was particularly pleased with the target he chose for his porcelain — a bee. The Latin for bee is of course Apis.)

We are told that this can save us from ourselves: obesity, risky driving, debt — all sorts of evils can be reduced by a bit of prestidigitation on our choices. But frankly, I wish our politicians would just nudge off. I resent the idea of politicians rigging our environment to make us do what they consider to be 'right'. What makes them think they know what is right for us? They do not even seem to trust half the population to pee straight without someone in authority showing them how. There is something disturbingly illiberal about governments trying to manipulate our behaviour without even revealing what they are up to, how they are doing it, or what result they hope to achieve. And with such a thin line separating bullying from nudging, I am sure that the politicians' initiatives will too often fall on the bullying side, even as they tell us they are on the nudging side. That point was brought home to me just days after news of the 'nudge' principle had come to the UK, when pinko professor Julian Le Grand suggested that smokers should be required to fill in a convoluted permit form before being allowed to buy cigarettes. (Why stop there, Julian? Why not make them get 'unclean' tattooed on their foreheads? That should 'nudge' a few in the 'right' direction. Something similar might 'nudge' people out of fast food joints too.) I fear that some people who call themselves liberals have scant idea of what freedom or liberty mean or are all about.

The database and surveillance state

Perhaps the rest of us do not understand it either. That is why we have drifted into a surveillance state and a bureaucratic state. The 'use of communications data' is permitted under the Regulation of Investigatory Powers Act 2000, which has given us a state surveillance system of record scale (though Elizabeth I maybe ran it close). Under it, government authorities, many hundreds of them, monitor our telephone calls and emails more than 500,000 times a year. Critics of the EU say it does not listen to people, but it does — specifically, under Project INDECT, it monitors citizens internet traffic, mobile phone calls, file sharing and much else.

Meanwhile, we are watched by about four million CCTV cameras — there are so many that nobody is exactly sure of the number — about a million of them in London. On the short half-mile walk down Victoria Street between Westminster Abbey and Westminster Cathedral, I counted a staggering 168 of them. Politicians and Home Office officials say their intrusive presence is justified on the grounds that they cut crime, but in fact they do not. The rapid spread of CCTV has gone hand in hand with rising crime, particularly violent crime. Often the images are not good enough, or have not been stored securely enough, to be used in court. According to the Metropolitan Police, only one crime is 'solved' for every 1,000 cameras. So why do we have them at all, snooping on us? I suspect, once again, it is mostly officials covering their backs. If a crime occurs and they have done nothing, they are in hot water. If they put up a camera, even if its images are unusable, as they mostly are, they can at least say they tried.

The database state is spreading, too. The Home Office seem very proud of their national DNA database, which is no surprise, since they have spent £300 million, the equivalent of 10,000 police salaries, developing it, to make it the largest DNA database in the world. This huge investment is probably why senior police officers have been ordered to continue logging the DNA of innocent people, despite a ruling from the European Court that around 850,000 records should be deleted. These belong mostly to people who were never tried nor convicted and so should be considered innocent.

DNA is very personal information, which the database puts at risk. The state's track record of ensuring the security of people's personal information is pathetic at best. Would *you* trust an organisation that lost two million names, addresses and bank account details in the mail?

From database state to information society
DNA is by no means the only information that the police hold on us, of course — information that is probably accessible to

any junior official, as those two million addresses were. They keep an eye on our car movements too. One of the leading lights from the think-tank Open Europe told me about the night they projected some eurosceptic light message onto the riverside front of Parliament a few years ago. It was harmless enough, but they were stopped and searched, of course. And they were also stopped every time their car crossed over one local police boundary into another.

In 2009 ministers 'downgraded' the multi-billion-pound ID card scheme from potentially compulsory to voluntary. So they say. In fact, the voluntary rollout was accelerated and the over-75s became the guinea pig group by being handed out ID cards for free. So they join the thousands of foreign nationals in the UK who will still be forced to carry one.

The trouble is that when you give state officials access to large amounts of your personal data, you never know how it will be used. A senior lawyer who was wrongly accused of forging a signature was questioned by the police and had her DNA swabbed; she was later sacked when a routine check by her firm revealed that she was on the national database. Nor can you ever be sure who is looking at your information; airport officials were caught using CCTV to ogle female passengers, and junior hospital doctors swapped juicy health records about various celebrities that came through their doors.

There is plenty of room on the ID database for many more kinds of data than those ministers wanted us to hand over, though. Indeed, the public service seems to collect data on us, on its own employees and on the routine details of its quotidian service. It helps make sure that everything, like the running of hospitals or care homes, for example, is run by the book and properly logged. But it drives out good people, who believe that these services should be based more on the personal well-being of their users, rather than on tick-box targets.

Jill Kirby, the energetic and level-headed Director of the Centre for Policy Studies, takes the view that we need to move from an oppressive database state to become a free, information technology society. IT should liberate us, and it should make it possible for us to do on a small scale, what previously has required the vast organisation of the state. We could, for example, have ownership and control of our own medical and school records, rather than this all being centrally managed. Information technology need not mean more and more power gravitating to the centre in the form of vast databases. We can use the technology to break the information stranglehold of the state, and to do things in our own, local, but well-informed way.

Reasserting our rights

There are certain obvious measures that a government that cares about this can do. For a start, we can scrap ID cards and the national identity database, and the child database ContactPoint — a particularly risky venture, given the poor security practices that surround most government databases. CRB checks too do more harm than good, balefully forcing a rift between public spirited adults and children, robbing kids of adult help and guidance, and making adults think they are somehow guilty until proven innocent — a status which sets the tone for how the police and other authorities then deal with us.

For the same reason, we should *not* keep DNA samples of innocent people, full stop. Again, the police argue that their hanging on to samples has allowed several serious crimes to be solved: but if we are interested in true justice we should be looking at the general effect rather than the specific cases, and the general effect is malign. Plainly, local authorities should not be able to access our communications data except in dire need.

There have been various other proposals: strengthening the office of the Information Commissioner and making it accountable to Parliament rather than the executive; taking the power to snoop on our calls and emails away from the Home Office and putting it under the protection of the Commissioner; curbing data sharing between government departments; and ensuring that no new laws or regulations are passed until their impact on the public's privacy is assessed and debated.

Like the erosion of our legal liberties, however, this problem requires more than a few legal amendments to sort it. Again, though I hate quangos I think it needs a full-scale year-long review to re-set the balance between the citizen and the state. I do not much like the idea of a bill of rights either — we have seen from the episode of the European Constitution that these things tend to become wish-lists for every vested interest group, rather than sets of rules that might restrain the power of our leaders; and our old 1689 Bill of Rights has not lasted the chill winds of centralising government too well in recent years, so a new one is unlikely to be any more immune. It might, however, be better than nothing, if it is indeed a statement of our rights and liberties, with a set of rules for protecting them against the mighty.

11

REGULATION

SETTING ENTERPRISE FREE AT LAST

Daniel Hannan is one of those rare creatures — a member of the European Parliament who has not been swallowed up by the system. Amazingly quick witted, erudite and focused, his speeches are always gripping. Indeed, his pithy and entertaining 'devalued prime minister of a devalued government' speech, which so embarrassed Gordon Brown on his visit to the European Parliament, has been viewed by over 2.5 million people.

Addressing a one-hundred-strong Adam Smith Institute reception taking place within spitting distance (literally) of the Treasury and the House of Commons, Hannan quickly brings his audience to attention. 'I have to tell you,' he begins, 'that some 84% of the laws in this country are now made in Brussels.' Then, after a pause: 'You don't look shocked enough. Let me tell you again. Some 84% of the laws in this country are now made in Brussels!' The point hits home.

In fact, the figure is probably an exaggeration — but not by much. It stems from a question asked of the German justice minister in the Bundestag a few years ago. His answer was that of the 23,167 legal acts adopted in Germany from

1998 to 2004, some 80% were of EU origin. And since EU legislation has grown in importance since then, political scientists extrapolated the figure to conclude that 84% of all German Laws originate in Brussels.

However, the think tank Open Europe did its own calculations, based not on *how much* EU regulation there was, but on the really important thing, *what it cost*. They sifted through more than 2,000 of the 'regulatory impact assessments' that Whitehall does on regulations these days, and found that 72% of the cost of laws and regulations over the last decade can be attributed to the European Union.

A figure of 72% is still shocking. It gets worse, of course (these things always do) once Whitehall has done its stuff, though, because of our civil servants' love of gold plating. Indeed, the TaxPayers Alliance calculates that, since 1997, Whitehall has added at least 7,700 pages of UK statutory instruments to prescribe exactly how EU directives are to be enforced. By the time EU rules have gone through the UK bureaucratic process, in other words, billions of pounds have been added on to their cost — billions that have to be paid by the public and businesses.

According to Gunther Verheugen, the EU Commissioner for Enterprise (which cannot be a particularly demanding job), the benefits of the EU single market are worth about €180 billion a year, while the cost of complying with all its regulation is about €600 billion a year. This does not seem to be a particularly good bang for the buck (or explosion for the euro, or whatever the appropriate phrase might be).

Putting limits on EU responsibilities
The steamroller progress of all this seems unstoppable. The Consumer Credit Directive, just to take one regulation, is not

even in force yet, but already the EU Commission is engaged on a 'post-implementation review' and pressing on with new legislative initiatives to extend it further. It is part of the deliberate attempt by the French and German governments to do down the UK's financial services sector, of course, and the UK rarely raises much of a voice against such things until everything is decided and it is far too late.

At the very least, we need a senior minister who is actually responsible for keeping an eye on what new regulatory longings are bringing a twinkle to French and German eyes, and doing something about it before things happen. Parliament too must scrutinise EU regulatory proposals far earlier than it does at the moment (if it ever scrutinises them at all).

Dan Hannan, of course, would like to go further. For his part, he would gladly set light to the bonfire of the *aquis communitaire*, the EU's amassed rule-book. 'Scrap the directives that tell us what hours we can work, what vitamins we can buy, how long we can sit on tractors, how loudly we can play our music,' he recommends. 'Return power to national governments, or better, to local authorities, or best of all, to individual citizens. Confine the EU to genuinely cross-border matters — tariff reduction, pollution, mutual product recognition. Member states should control everything else — agriculture and fisheries, criminal justice, and social and employment policy.' He is not optimistic it will ever happen, of course: too many eurocrats would lose their jobs.

The burden on business — and on us
The trouble is that while this regulatory roundabout continues spinning, the rest of us are losing *our* jobs. And it is not just the costs that the EU imposes on us — it is the

other 28% that we impose on ourselves too. The British Chambers of Commerce (BCC) publishes what it calls an annual 'barometer' of regulation, which shows that the pressure on business is rising and rising. The cumulative cost of regulations on business since 1998, they say, has now reached a staggering £77 billion. (Mind you, across the whole of Europe, they figure that regulations cost EU businesses about €1 trillion, roughly an eighth of the EU's GDP.)

There are data protection regulations, groundwater policies, regulations on how many hours people can work, tax credit regulations, directives on part-time workers, water supply regulations, instructions on the use of pesticides, disability legislation, recycling and waste controls, parental leave, building regulations, standards for the energy efficiency of stoves and machines, pension scheme rules, flexible working requirements, limits on what sort of waste you can burn (not cardboard, unfortunately), home information packs, weights and measures stuff, freedom of information obligations, CRB vetting of employees, work permits and ID cards for foreign workers, laws to stop money laundering, time off for training rules, various pollution standards, commands on renewable energy, arrangements for consulting employees, regulations to prevent discrimination, numerous accounting regulations (none of which the government's own national accounts would pass) and of course a large body of health and safety regulation, including a book of instructions on how to use a ladder.

All very worthy objectives, no doubt: but my, how the cost mounts up. If you are running a firm, you need an army of compliance officers to deal with all this stuff. If you are a bank or a financial firm that actually takes people's money, you need even more. The cost of it all means that small firms cannot survive, which is why the banks and others have grown bigger and bigger, until — having grown too big to be allowed to fail — they have the taxpayer over a barrel. The same sort of thing is happening in other sectors too: it all squeezes out competition, makes the market less open and more monopolistic and leaves the customer with a much worse deal.

The sources of regulation
Apart from Brussels, obviously, where does all this stuff come from? According to Tim Ambler and Keith Boyfield in their 2005 Adam Smith Institute report *Roadmap to Reform: Deregulation*, there are three sources. There is, of course, the European Commission which pumps out regulations, which have the force of law across the EU, and directives (which EU countries have to work out for themselves how to put into effect). Second, there is Whitehall, which delights in gold-plating all these directives and then comes up with a large number of new regulations of its own. Third, there are the UK regulatory offices themselves — the folk who make the rules for privatised utilities like gas, water, electricity, rail and telephones, or who try to stop us discriminating against minorities, or who tell the banks how quickly they have to pick up the phone when their customers call.

It is a sad fact of life that regulation is usually counterproductive, and the net effect of it is usually malign. Business complains that the focus of regulation is always on stopping things, or on providing redress to customers who have been short-changed, rather than on creating an environment in which trade, enterprise and innovation can flourish and grow. The whole business is highly political: something happens

and then the politicians launch a whole process of announcements, press releases, tip-offs, focus groups, polls, podcasts,
speeches, statements and parliamentary questions all
reassuring the public that they are acting to make sure we are
all well protected by their intended reforms — without one
word of advice, opinion or consultation from the businesses
who might be affected.

'Just one stray word from a minister can have a huge
impact on our share price and the value of our business,' one
board director of one of the top 100 UK companies told me.
'It means we are constantly having to try to figure out what
reality lies behind the spin — if there is any there at all. So
we find ourselves being led up lots of blind alleys, before
ministers move on to something else, their noisy statements
subside and their ideas are quietly watered down or forgotten
entirely. It is a huge drain of energy and resources. Sadly, it
is the customers who end up paying for it all.' Perhaps the
government has taken his point, though their proposed new
'consultation on consultations' hardly seems the best way to
deal with it.

'Another problem,' my friend continues (get businesspeople on this subject and your ears will be pinned back for
hours), 'is that so much regulation is so ill-defined. In our
industry, finance, for example, we are told that our lending to
customers must be 'sustainable' and 'affordable'. Parliament
never rules what these mean, it is all down to the interpreta-
tion of officials. Often the ruling will be retrospective: if
somebody cannot repay their loan, they will ask officials to
rule that the agreement they signed was not based on 'proper'
advice or was not a 'reasonable' contract. So lenders like us
try to stay clearly on the right side of the line — wherever it
is — with the result that we cannot risk lending to poorer

people, and lend only to better-off ones who we know can 'afford' to borrow as much as they want. So when a factory closes and a lot of poorly-paid workers are laid off, they find they cannot get loans to tide them over because we face the risk of officials declaring our loans to them 'unsustainable'. Exactly who is regulation supposed to be helping? I thought it was there to help the most vulnerable.'

Regulations tax the poor
The poorest are hurt more directly by regulations, too. The obligation for energy companies to put money into renewable energy, for example, along with the 'climate change levy' puts 14% on the cost of electricity bills, which poorer people can hardly afford — especially since utility bills eat up a large proportion of their household budget, around half of it in the case of people on benefit. It is not even as if all these wind factories are even economic — they only exist because of the regulation and the amount of money that the power companies are obliged to spend on them, and even then they will only last fifteen years or so before we will have to replace them. Nor is our national interest at stake. There might be a case for us all paying to make ourselves secure against the Russians deciding to turn off our gas supplies, or for research into new forms of clean energy: but there is no moral justification at all for making the poor pay more for their electricity so as to put up expensive, unsightly, uneconomic, bronchitic, short-lived wind turbines.

Meanwhile, on top of this (yes, you guessed, it gets worse), our electricity bills will have to rise by £200 billion between now and 2020 just to meet new EU regulatory standards. And (yes, worse still) EU water regulations mean our bills will rise by another £100 billion to meet those too.

It all amounts to a massive tax on poor people for the benefit of rich utility companies.

Regulation is easier than deregulation
The trouble is that it is much easier to regulate than to deregulate. Regulation has lots of advantages for politicians. If they do nothing, and people fall off stepladders, they will face criticism that they should have prevented this awful occurrence. If they publish a guide on the use of stepladders, and bring in rules on the size and manufacture of stepladders, and laws that people may not use stepladders without rigorous advance training, then students in the Bodleian library may not be able to reach their books any more, but at least the politicians can say that they did their best to keep us all safe.

Encrustations of regulation are hard to prise off the rock of free enterprise because every one is there for a reason. The reason may be public spirited, like the desire to prevent injury to people working at heights. Or it might be purely self-regarding, like the desire to avoid blame by saying you laid down rules. It might even just be ministers trying to show colleagues that they are active and should get a promotion. Whatever the reason, you can be sure that somebody, somewhere, sometime, thought that the regulation was a good idea, and has persuaded others of the same.

When you suggest that some regulation should go, therefore, you are greeted with howls of outrage. Do you *really* want people to climb stepladders even though they have *no training*? Pass me the smelling salts! Can you possibly *live* with the thought that you had personally left some unfortunate person crippled because you did not lay down rules about how stepladders should be used? It is no good saying that we would live in a better world if we all used a bit of common sense rather than tried to swathe ourselves in cotton wool. It takes only one injury, and you have lost the moral argument.

This is why all government attempts to 'cut red tape' or to create 'better regulation' through a raft of initiatives, task forces, quangos and committees have been a failure. True, regulations are of slightly better quality than they once were, and the supporting documentation about their impact is an improvement. In terms of their number and cost, though, the three sources of regulation — the EU, Whitehall and the regulators themselves — just keep churning out the stuff.

More tailored solutions
Ambler and Boyfield argue that we need a much more tailored approach to cutting the regulatory cloth. For each of the three sources of regulation, we need to look, they say, at three different deregulatory strategies. First, we need to prevent unnecessary new regulations being born in the first place. Second, we need to pare back and consolidate the existing regulations. Third, we need to be more sensible and proportionate when it comes to compliance and inspection, and in the cost that all this imposes on individuals and businesses.

On top of this, we should not have more than one level of government regulating the same issue. Tim Ambler, who as the former finance director of a top stock market company and fellow of the London Business School knows a thing or two about regulation, takes the view that the growth in the *proportion* of regulation that comes from the EU is not surprising or worrying, since many of the issues that are growing in importance are cross-border issues, such as tariffs, trade and the environment. As long as they are enforced uniformly across member countries so as to create a genuinely open market without differences in standards between different places, we should not be concerned. What is alarming, though, is not the proportion but the *volume* of regulation coming from each of the three sources, and the fact that we have more than one level of government regulating the same issue. We do not need Whitehall and Brussels both trying to second-guess the other.

Ambler's wily plan is to demand that the EU should stop issuing directives and instead issue only regulations. Directives are simply framework laws that provide national flexibility about exactly *how* the framework principle should be implemented in each country. Maybe it is a cunning ruse to swamp the UK with regulation, because they know that our assiduous civil service will gold plate the lot, adding to the burden on our businesses, while other countries will leave them as bare metal, leaving their own firms with a comparative advantage. What the UK should do, instead, is to push for all EU rules to appear as regulations, finished laws that have to apply equally in all countries, just as they stand. The howls of outrage from a number of EU countries would surely temper the zeal of the regulatory enthusiasts.

Seeing the wood for the trees
Of course, there are so many regulations coming through Parliament — they go through in the form of statutory instruments, so do not need debate — that most MPs never even look at them, much less oppose them. (Anyone who did would face an immediate backlash from their whips and colleagues, who do not want to hang around until midnight in order to debate the issue.) It all means that a few critical and

important — but potentially controversial — new rules get nodded through, lost in the forest of tiny changes. Ambler suggests that they should instead be rated or ranked in terms of their importance, so MPs could see instantly if they were worth reading and maybe even worth objecting to.

There are perhaps three hundred regulations that impose a significant burden, such as the Plastic Materials And Articles In Contact With Food (England) Regulations 2009. The other three thousand or so are minor administrative orders about, say, parking restrictions in Derbyshire. Just putting the two on different coloured paper would help MPs to know what they should actually be looking at, and which can be just nodded through.

Another critical move, thinks Ambler, is for the UK to be challenging EU regulation earlier. The House of Commons has a European Scrutiny Committee, but it generally deals with things long after it is too late. The quango that is supposed to scrutinise new regulations, the Better Regulation Executive, should also challenge regulations earlier and more forcefully, but in practice it is far weaker and far less prompt. Again, perhaps the House of Lords, duly reconstituted, could provide an early warning system, and even a filter.

Is your regulation really necessary?

Like the 'Is your quango really necessary?' posters I suggested, we could use some asking 'Is your *regulation* really necessary?' too.

At the very least, there should be an obligation on parliamentarians and ministers to consider any possible alternatives to regulation. Perhaps insurance would be a better way of reducing the unnecessary risks that people take at work or at home, for example; and perhaps cutting back rules that stop the insurance market from working properly would be more cost-effective than imposing new regulatory burdens on everyone else. Or again, the cheapest strategy might be simply to require that firms educate employees about managing their risk, rather than specifying in detail how they should do it.

Then again, the best solution should be to face down the interest groups calling for more regulation, and do nothing. However well intentioned various political initiatives might be, a 2009 report by the National Audit Office concluded that initiativitis was most of the problem, and that the biggest burden on business was the constant *change* in regulations. We should focus on setting minimum standards and sticking to them, rather than changing the rules all the time.

One good way to break the habit would be to introduce no new statutory instruments (apart from those required for EU law) for a whole year, giving time for a robust new system to be developed and for civil servants to be trained to use it. If something is important enough to need to go through Parliament, it should go through overtly, as a piece of primary legislation that is debated in both houses, not as secondary legislation that is just nodded through without even being looked at.

During that year, we could whittle down a few more quangos, like the Regulatory Policy Committee and the Local Better Regulation Office (whose website says its aim is to 'reduce unnecessary red tape' but which is, in fact, part of it). The Better Regulation Executive should be quite sufficient to make sure that, when new regulatory proposals start trickling through again, they (and alternatives to them) are scrutinised and evaluated.

Consolidating and paring back

When it comes to existing EU regulation, there is plainly plenty of scope for boiling down the 20,000-odd pages of *acquis communitaire*. It should be reviewed, consolidated and simplified, particularly the costly rules on labour markets. In fact, EU legislation has sometimes helped simplify the existing UK regulations that it partly supersedes. A good example is the Regulatory Reform (Fire Safety) Order 2005, which replaced over seventy pieces of EU and UK fire safety orders.

Apart from just tidying up and consolidating the existing rules, however, we also need to pare back the number and burden of regulations. A good way to do this is government department by government department, as in New Zealand. In the UK context, the focus should be on asking why we have regulations that the rest of the EU seem quite content to do without. Departments should be given a deadline to scrap all their regulations, except those demanded by EU law — or be prepared to have a rigorous debate on what they want to keep. The Better Regulation Executive could go through each department, taking on the role of wrecking crew.

Limits on government departments

Various other methods of culling burdensome regulations have been mooted, but none of them are remotely easy to do. One suggestion which Neil O'Brien of the Institute of Directors seemed to favour is the 'one in, one out' rule (or even better, a 'one in, two out' rule), by which departments would only be allowed to introduce a new regulation if they scrapped existing ones. Of course, they would scrap the most unimportant and obscure little regulations, but even that would be a positive step. Better, though, would be to clear all the junk out first, so that departments would be facing a genuinely difficult choice.

A variant on this is a 'regulatory budget' under which departments can only add to the cost burden on business by cutting other regulations that impose at least equal costs. That raises problems, because some departments will be responsible for a number of costly EU regulations that they cannot get out of, unlike others. And whether we can trust departmental ministers and officials to make a fair assessment of the costs of the regulations is open to question. O'Brien suggests another model, that of British Columbia, where the 'budget' you aim to reduce is not the cost of the regulations, but the number of lines on the various forms. A crude measure, right enough, but if we are out to cut red tape, the idea seems promising.

Other people have suggested a sort of 'star chamber' of senior politicians who will comb through the body of regulation and regulatory proposals and decide which ones can be lost. In practice these have never worked well. Throwing out a regulation, or a proposal for a regulation, is a slight to the relevant minister — and ministers are after all colleagues, so the temptation is to preserve friendships and let the regulations stay or the proposals go through.

Sunset laws are another option. The idea here is that regulations (and quangos) are set up with only a limited life. They will expire automatically after, say, three or five years if they are not consciously renewed by Parliament. It is an idea that we should certainly pursue, though I am not optimistic that it will bear fruit. Back in 1997, Tony Blair promised to bring in sunset laws on regulations, but he did not deliver any, except in about two specific cases. The reason was that ministers always hate the idea. After struggling to get regulations in place, three years later they have to do it all again. That is not something that appeals to politicians: they want to mess up one part of our lives, then move on to mess up the rest of it.

Focus on regulators

Tim Ambler, who always manages a cheery smile even when he is sticking the knife in to the quangocracy, says that we should focus less on regulation, and more on the regulators who enforce them (and indeed cause a lot of them). Our regulators, he says, should be independent of the executive, and should therefore be accountable directly to Parliament, and not to ministers.

They should also focus on their proper role, that of 'economic' regulation — in other words, trying to make regulated businesses like the privatised utilities deliver better value for customers — rather than trying to impose ministers' political agenda on them. Extending competition, or even trying to mimic what open competition would do — that is, forcing down prices and forcing up service quality — is one thing. Making utilities pick up the cost of maintaining service to people who cannot or will not pay their bills, however, is not economics but civics, and something that should be paid for overtly through the welfare budget.

Ideally, though, regulators should stop pretending to be competition and give us a dose of the real thing. Their target should be to phase themselves out and to phase more and more competition in. When I learnt economics at university (though that was so long ago they still called it 'political philosophy'), I was taught that competition in telephones was theoretically impossible. Telephones were a natural monopoly. Well, they are not any more, of course: almost every developed country has literally dozens of competing operators. New technologies, and new ideas from across the planet, can work out ways of injecting competition into most things, from railways to gas supply to water. Extending competition is what our regulators should be focusing on: not the minute details of the regulated companies' cost structures. When they have extended competition as far as they can and faded away, the Competition Commission is surely sufficient to mop up any remaining issues.

Setting enterprise free

Regulation, though, is something that large companies love, because the sheer cost of complying with it keeps out their competition. It is time to reverse the balance. We should take small companies out of regulation entirely. Italy did something like this, deregulating its so-called 'small artisan' sector.

We need to make it possible for one person to hire another without going through all the rigmarole of PAYE, national insurance, and labour law. Do small businesses really need to keep accounts in detailed ways specified by the regulators (and designed by accountants, who will of course profit from it), when they probably have a keener grasp on their daily cash flow than anyone else? It is time to liberate small firms, and allow them to do their job and create jobs. Hours of work, pay, even anti-discrimination rules, parental leave and the lengthy procedures on redundancy — we should scrap them all.

Some people will say that this leaves employees of small companies unprotected. At the moment, however, that protection is coming at the cost of their jobs. Small firms have to be flexible and if they are to survive, they cannot be hidebound by a one-size-fits-all system of regulatory rules. Small firms are also more personal enterprises: their bosses are not going to take advantage of the lack of regulation on them to cheat their employees or expose their employees to risk, because the employees and the bosses are friends and see themselves as colleagues. And if they do fall out — well, studies show that regulation (rather than taxation) is the biggest obstacle to economic growth, and with lighter regulation in the small business sector, we can be pretty sure that many more job opportunities will become available.

It is a point that will not be lost on those who are struggling to get themselves off social benefits either.

12

TAXES

'In this world,' wrote the American founding father Benjamin Franklin, 'nothing is certain but death and taxes.' Unfortunately, they come in the wrong order. Franklin and his revolutionary friends used to complain about 'taxation without representation'; but those of us living in the UK today may feel that taxation *with* representation is not all that hot either.

Tax Freedom Day

As the political class taps deeper and deeper into our net income in order to fuel its gross habits, the tax burden has risen and risen. Perhaps the simplest measure of it is Tax Freedom Day, which the Adam Smith Institute calculates each year. Tax Freedom Day is that point of the year when we have finally earned enough to pay off the demands of the tax collectors and at last start working for ourselves. If government takes a third of the nation's income in taxes, for example, that means that Tax Freedom Day comes a third of the way through the year, four months deep, around the end of April.

Does working four months of the year just to pay taxes

seem a lot? Well dream on, because our taxes have not been
that low in four decades. Back in 1965 — the year of
Churchill's state funeral, an escalation of the Vietnam war,
and the Beatles topping the charts for eleven weeks with
Ticket To Ride, *Help!* and *Day Tripper* — Tax Freedom Day
fell on 27 April. The following year (1966, when England
won the World Cup), Harold Wilson as prime minister and
Denis Healey as Chancellor of the Exchequer were making
us work a week longer to support their expanding
government, until 4 May. They gave us an additional twelve
days hard labour the next year, then another six the next,
seven more the next, then another four the next. By 1970,
when the pair left office, Tax Freedom Day fell on 2 June, a
full five weeks later than it had been when they came to
power.

For most of the Blair years, Tax Freedom Day hovered
around the end of May. Tax Freedom Day 2009 was
remarkable in that it came a fortnight earlier, on 14 May, the
earliest since 1973, when Slade dominated the charts with
Cum On Feel The Noize (spelling was never their strong
point), *Skweeze Me Pleeze Me* and the perennial *Merry Xmas
Everybody*. But then in addition to the government making us
work 134 days of the year for them, they also borrowed
wildly, loading another seven weeks' worth of debt onto us,
which would take Tax Freedom Day to 25 June, the highest
burden in a generation.

Stealth taxes

The French finance minister Colbert talked of the art of
taxation as plucking the most feathers from the goose with
the least hissing. Gordon Brown surpassed that. With his
stealth taxes, people did not even know they were being

plucked.

Within weeks of taking office, he put a secret £5 billion tax on pensions, and taxed health insurance and mortgages. Next year, he taxed travel insurance and foreign investments. In 1999 he sneaked up national insurance contributions and taxed workplace training. Then he froze various tax thresholds so that inflation alone caused people to end up paying more tax without realising it.

After that came extra council tax on second homes, a charge for submitting your tax form late, a 'victims fund' levy on everyone using the courts, taxes on nursery schools and school buses, a doubling of the cost of passports, a 'lighthouse tax' on boats, rises in air passenger duty (or skyway robbery, as it is known), extra taxes on fishing licences, higher NHS dentistry charges, hospital car park fees, new taxes on premium bonds, a twenty-fold rise in the cost of pub and restaurant licences, litter taxes on takeaways, council tax increases on houses with a nice view, new vehicle registration fees, charges to have your wheelie-bins delivered, new duties on longer vehicles, and of course a massive increase in the number of revenue-generating speed cameras.

Byzantine complexity
Not only is tax higher, it has grown more complicated too. *Tolley's Tax Guide*, which accountants use to work out how much tax we all owe, is now 10,134 pages long which I figure is seven times the size of *War And Peace*.

Complexity raises four problems. First, it forces individuals and companies to employ expensive accountants to guide them through the tax code and make sure they are complying with all the rules properly. Second, the more byzantine the rules, the greater is your chance of making a mistake. Often, Revenue & Customs will take businesses to court because neither of them understands exactly what the rules mean. But that just loads cost and uncertainty on businesses.

Third, when taxes are high and complicated, a huge amount of human energy goes into finding those little nooks in the tax code that will reduce your tax bill — energy that could have been spent on producing something more useful. Friends and I once started a small business, but most of our early discussions revolved around how to structure the business tax-efficiently, rather than what we were actually going to produce. I am sure that the same sort of thing still happens in almost every business start-up. What a complete waste of talent!

Fourth — and most subtle but most pernicious — all this turns the taxed and the tax collectors into adversaries. Revenue & Customs come to believe that we are all on the fiddle, trying to find ways to keep our cash from them. Taxpayers see tax officials as unfairly trying to get as much as possible out of them so they qualify for bigger bonuses. Neither side trusts the other. Like the police, sadly, we no longer see tax officers as serving the public, but as serving the state.

Blue-pencilling the tax form

'If — as the politicians of all parties seem to agree — economic growth is the only realistic way out of our financial hole, then high and complicated taxes are not going to help,' says the Senior Lecturer in Tax Law at Bournemouth University, Richard Teather. He should know. In addition to his day job, he is also a prolific writer and commentator on tax issues. Companies, institutions, even countries, come to him for advice.

You will often see Richard (sporting one of his extensive collection of waistcoats) at Westminster discussions on tax policy, including meetings of the Adam Smith Institute, where he is Senior Tax Fellow. 'The online tax form looks simple enough,' he tells me, 'but it is a sleight-of-hand by Revenue & Customs. When you actually delve into each section, there are pages and pages of hidden details for taxpayers to wade through.'

It is no wonder that millions of us cannot navigate through a tax form without professional accountants to guide us. One leading firm, KPMG, calculated the total administrative burden of our taxes at a staggering £5.1 billion a year, a burden our economy could well do without.

You always used to recognise civil servants by their blue tongues. That is because they were issued with special pencils — which looked and worked just like ordinary pencils, until you licked the lead, which then turned blue and left an ineradicable mark on the paper you were working on. The Lord Chancellor famously used one when censoring stage plays, so that his crossings-out could not be erased by theatre producers — giving rise to the description 'blue' for a play that carried a large number of such cuts.

It is time to appoint a new sort of Lord Chancellor, a senior figure in charge of blue-pencilling large parts of the tax code. Start with the actual tax forms that businesses, employers and individuals get each year. How many lines can we take out? How many hundred pages of rules are there hidden behind each line? And how many thousands of civil servants does it take to enforce those rules?

Preening Chancellors, lost jobs

One reason why tax is so taxing is just human nature. If you become Chancellor, Budget Day is your one big moment. All eyes, and hundreds of television cameras, are focused on you, on your red box, on your body language at the dispatch box, even what drink you fortify yourself with during your speech. The desire to milk the occasion for everything it is worth is overpowering. So you pull rabbits out of the hat: a new programme here, new help to some group there, a concession to others elsewhere. At the end of your speech, you may have added hundreds more pages to the tax code; but people will not judge you on that. They will judge you on who you have made better or worse off. They will judge you not on your economics, but on your politics.

It may be asking a lot for a Chancellor to simplify or reduce taxes, but right now it is essential. High and complicated taxes are a burden on businesses — particularly on small and growing businesses, which are the ones that will create the jobs that will pull us through our financial doldrums. The US Census Bureau says that nearly all job creation in America comes from firms less than five years old, a result confirmed by a recent Kaufmann Foundation report. The same is true in the UK.

If you tax something you will get less of it; but here we are, blithely taxing people when they work, when they save, when they build up productive capital, when they run businesses that serve the public, when they employ people and when they pass on their wealth to others. These are all things we want to encourage; yet we tax them. It is barmy.

A quagmire of rates and reliefs

The World Economic Forum currently ranks us 84th out of

133 countries in terms of how attractive (or otherwise) their tax system makes them. Even Chancellors are aware of the disincentive effects of high and complicated taxes, and over the years they sought to reduce the number of different income tax bands. Quite recently, there were just two, a 20p standard rate and a 40p rate on higher incomes. But it has got complicated again. Gordon Brown introduced a 10p starting rate; and now we have a 50p rate on incomes over £150,000, leaving us with four different bands — though if you are a foreigner or work for a bank that pays you a bonus, you face other taxes too.

Meanwhile there are tax-free allowances of different sizes for blind people and married couples. There is the 'age allowance' for folk aged between 65 and 75, and another for those over 75 — except that the more you earn, the less allowance you get, so it is hard for most people to work out. There are also reliefs for pension contributions, except for people earning more than £150,000. (This has the bizarre result that if you earn £170,000 and put £20,000 into a pension you get no tax kickback, but if you earn £150,000 and your employer puts £20,000 in for you, you do. But it is these little quirks that keep tax advisers cheerful.)

You and your employer also pay national insurance, which is subject to different tax-free allowances for different people, and if you earn a lot you lose even those. The rates you pay depend on whether you are married, self employed, contracted into a private pension, and probably your hair colour too. It all means that not even Revenue & Customs know for sure what amount of tax different people should pay, according to Gabriel Stein of financial analysts Lombard Street Research. He thinks that many of us will pay our tax bill in good faith, only for Revenue & Customs to come back to us later and demand more money because they got our tax calculation wrong. It is a confusing, time-consuming, costly mess.

In 2009 the Conservatives committed themselves to a two-year national insurance holiday for small firms, recognising that the administrative burden it places on them is disproportionately high — around three-quarters of the cost of complying with income tax and national insurance falls on the smallest third of all businesses. George Osborne claimed this would save 60,000 jobs. Perhaps: but it would be better to explore ways of ending this tax on jobs — a tax on jobs that a business has to pay whether it is making a profit or a loss — permanently, not just for two years.

Ending complexity and bringing choice into NI

National insurance was dreamed up as a compulsory social insurance premium for things like the NHS. It was not a flat amount like most insurance premiums, and higher earners paid more — but only within set limits. Recently, the top-end limit has been removed– another stealth tax aimed at 'the rich' — and national insurance has become pretty much just another income tax, albeit a stealth tax, since it is deducted by employers.

The sensible thing to do would be to merge the two, and spare us all huge complication; but no politician would do that. It would make the UK's taxes look too high — a starting rate that took a third of people's income, and a top rate that snaffled two-thirds of it. The politicians know it would be suicide to make that reality too obvious. As a tax which brings in 17% of government revenue, second only to income tax, the politicians like national insurance just where it is — hidden from the public because it is employers who pay the bulk of it.

Even if no politician will simply roll national insurance into the headline rate of income tax, they could at least make it subject to the same rules and allowances, which would cut down the administrative burden for businesses and individuals. As my colleague Madsen Pirie suggests in his 2009 Adam Smith Institute book *Zero Base Policy*, it could still be separated out as a 'social insurance premium', perhaps. Whatever the presentational fiction, the reality of the streamlining would still save jobs.

But is national insurance an insurance premium, or a tax? If it is insurance, covering the NHS and other social benefits, we could allow people to opt out of it and make their own arrangements instead, if they thought some other insurer could do better than the state. That would give the state's health and social insurance plans some useful competition (along the lines of, say, the health system in the Netherlands or pensions in Sweden), promoting innovation and better customer service. Allowing people to take their national insurance contributions and divert them towards competing insurers of their own choice would revolutionise the provision of healthcare and insurances for disability, unemployment, and other misfortunes.

The truth, though, is that national insurance is a mixture of tax and social insurance. We should separate out these elements, adding the tax element to taxation, but allow people to take the genuine insurance contribution to a private insurer if they choose. The calculation might be complicated, but the benefits in terms of providing real alternatives to state health and welfare, and opening up choice for individuals, are truly enormous.

Simpler, flatter income taxes

The combination of high taxes and impenetrable complexity
has led more and more countries to adopt lower and simpler
taxes — sometimes as simple as having just one rate, a so-
called 'flat tax'.

The core principle of the flat tax is that everybody pays
the same. There are no complicated rate bands under which
some people pay a higher rate than others. All or most of the
complicated concessions and allowances are swept away. So
it is perfectly clear what everyone should be paying, and you
do not need an accounting degree to work it out.

The idea has been adopted by about twenty countries,
including several EU members. The prosperous Asian tigers
of Hong Kong and Singapore have had something like a flat
tax for many years, but the Baltic state of Estonia first
brought the idea to Europe in 1994, replacing three rates on
personal income, and another on company profits, with one
uniform 26% rate. With the boost it gave to economic
growth, Estonia never looked back. Before long its EU
neighbours Latvia and Lithuania copied it. Another EU
country, Slovakia, brought in a 19% rate on personal and
company incomes, and foreign investment flooded in. The
Czech Republic has a flat tax. The majority party in Poland
is considering a 15% flat tax. And so it continues.

In 2001, Russia introduced a flat rate of 19% on personal
income (prompting the Estonians to cut their own rate to
match). Further east, Serbia went for a 14% flat tax in 2003,
Ukraine a 13% rate a year later, and in 2005, Georgia with
12% and Romania with 16%.

What makes the flat tax idea so attractive to so many
countries? It may just be that they are fed up with unfathomable tax complexity of the sort we have in the UK. With

only one rate, tax becomes far simpler — all the more so if existing reliefs are cut back too. That reduces administrative costs not just for the government, but for individuals and those all-important small businesses.

A flat tax cuts down avoidance and evasion, too. Because the rules are simpler, there are fewer loopholes — and if the rate is low, it is less worthwhile trying to avoid tax anyway. In the UK, Revenue & Customs reckon that £40 billion a year — around a twelfth of the total tax take — goes uncollected every year thanks to mistakes, evasion and people avoiding tax by exploiting various loopholes. With a flat tax, there would be fewer hiding places — and less need for them — and far less cash would go walkabout.

Furthermore, low and flat taxes do not distort people's financial decisions so much. In the UK, almost everyone decides what to save or invest largely on the basis of tax rates and concessions, but with a flat tax, people make these decisions for the right reasons — whether they make economic sense.

A flat tax for the UK?
In Britain, a working proposal for a flat income tax might have a single uniform rate of 20% (equal to the current standard rate). We do not want the poorest families to face this burden, though, so we should exempt everyone below the minimum wage rate (about £12,000) from paying tax at all. Most flat tax systems have generous low-income allowances like this. Politicians can then seek applause, not on the basis of some minor change in rates or thresholds, but on the much more meaningful figure of how many millions of people they have taken out of tax entirely.

Of course, if we lower the tax rate and double the tax-free

threshold to £12,000, Revenue & Customs would rake in less money from us — about £26 billion, they reckon. Yet it might not be quite that high, because we could also get rid of lots of concessions, like tax reliefs for Individual Savings Accounts (ISAs) and pension contributions, business credits for research and development, and tax exemptions on certain state benefits. When tax rates are high, people guard such concessions jealously. When rates are low, they are of little value to anyone.

That simplicity makes the flat tax a doddle to collect. You can fire most Revenue & Customs staff. You simply ask employers how much they pay to workers above £12,000, and send them a bill for 20% of it. Job done.

As well as cutting bureaucracy, though, there is no doubt too that low taxes will promote economic growth and create jobs, generating higher tax revenues in the process. There would be far less avoidance and evasion. And investing in the UK would become more attractive, so new capital would flow in.

Indeed, economists think that the higher economic growth and easier collection would see tax revenues recovering in just three years — in other words, within the lifetime of a Parliament.

Soak the rich: cut taxes!
Intuitively, you might think that a flat tax would help only the rich, who would pay a lower rate. But when rates are lower, people have less incentive for avoiding or evading tax, or for moving themselves or their money abroad. And the evidence is clear that with lower rates, the rich end up paying more.

During the 1980s, the Thatcher government cut the top rate of tax from 83% to 40% — and higher earners did indeed pay more. The top tenth of earners went from paying a 35% share of total revenues collected in 1979, to 42% of total revenues in 1990.

The United States found the same during its four tax-cutting episodes: 1921–26 (when the top rate fell from 63% to 25%); 1964 (when Kennedy cut top rates from 91% to 70%); 1981–84 (the Reagan tax cuts); and 2001–03 (the Bush tax cuts). Each time, total revenues rose, and the rich paid more of the total.

But lower rates help the poor too. Getting into work becomes a much better option for people on social benefits when they no longer face 90% effective tax rates. And that mean means large chunks of our complex tax credit system can go too.

Bizarrely, the Treasury does not consider these incentive effects of tax changes. It suggests that if you put tax rates up by 10%, you will get 10% more revenue. By that reckoning, raising income tax to 100% should net the government twice the cash it gets today. In reality, though, the entire working population would leave the country. The Treasury should switch to what economists call 'dynamic modelling' — in other words, deciding tax rates on the basis of how people might actually react to them.

Getting there

With radical tax reduction and simplification, we can speed up Britain's economic recovery, get people out of the benefits trap, and make all taxpayers — rich and poor — better off. It seems like a policy that politicians should be exploring with much greater urgency.

As Madsen Pirie says, one way of creating a flat tax would simply be to increase, year by year, the higher rate tax threshold — the amount of money you have to earn before you pay the top income tax rates. Eventually, nearly everyone would be under that amount, paying only 20%. Then you can just scrap the higher rate entirely and — *voila!* — you have a 20% flat tax.

Taxes on savings

A penny saved is a penny taxed. The money you save into the bank comes out of your taxed income. On top of that, you pay tax on any interest you earn on it. Put it into an annuity that will give you a regular income as long as you live, and you pay tax on that too. That is why the only tax relief that Richard Teather would spare is the tax incentive for people to save into ISAs. We have to have *some* encouragement to do the right thing.

However, taxing savings at every stage is easy, which is why our government authorities do it. Yet it is counterproductive, since saving is the source of funds for investment in UK industry and economic growth. That does not just mean funds that are saved with banks or pension companies, which they then lend out to businesses. David Green, head of the civil society think-tank Civitas, points out that many — or perhaps most — of the most innovative businesses, like Apple or Microsoft, have not been built on the back of bank loans. Banks typically cannot understand them and think them too risky. Rather, they have been built on the foundation of loans provided by family members. We need families to save if we are to see radical innovation flourish.

Logically, says Richard, we would not tax savings or interest at all, until they are actually drawn as income. This used to be the case with workplace pensions, but that has all gone now: the tax reliefs on what you put in have been tightened, there is a stealth tax on the growth of your savings, and you still pay when you draw your pension. So your savings are being taxed when they go in to your pension pot, when they are there, and when you take them out again. It all leaves the ISA model, where you can at least squirrel away a modest amount tax-free, as the only way that the tax system actually encourages saving.

As for pensions, we now have about thirty-five different tax arrangements on different sorts of pensions. Too often, governments promise to create 'simpler' arrangements, but — because you cannot simply tear up people's long-term pension contracts — they end up merely adding some new system to the thirty-something that already exist. Any new 'simpler' pension plan would do precisely the same, but if it really was simple and intelligible enough, it might well eclipse all the others. Perhaps the most straightforward idea is for the government to match what people save into a pension — a BOGOF (buy one, get one free) plan. That would be easy, would encourage saving for retirement (and so help keep retired people off state benefits) and would be a pension plan that people could actually understand and see the advantage of.

Company and capital taxes

Companies pay tax as well as individuals. So if you maybe bought some privatised company shares and still get dividends from them, you will find yourself paying tax on money that has, in fact, already been taxed.

The tax on companies, corporation tax, started as a simple tax on profits. But by massaging their costs (like spending on equipment), companies could reduce their profit figures, and therefore their tax bill. Naturally the tax authorities have fought this bitterly over the years, adding more and more pages of rules onto the tax code in order to stop it — leaving corporation tax hugely complicated.

Corporation tax is also high. Our rate is higher than the average of the developed countries, the OECD; higher than the EU average; higher than the world average; and much higher than the rates charged by the new EU countries of eastern Europe. Already, several companies have relocated to Ireland — conveniently nearby, English-speaking, but with a corporation tax rate half of ours.

In 2007 the Centre for Economic and Business Research worked out what would be the effect on the UK of cutting its corporation tax rate to Ireland's level. By 2021, they concluded, such a cut would have raised GDP by 8.7%, increased investment by 60% and added 9% to wages and employment.

If the UK is going to recover economically, it can only be by trading our way out. With the pound low, it is a good time to be selling our wares around the globe. Business, not government, will pull us out of our debt hole. So anything we can do to encourage business growth, innovation, and start-ups should be welcome.

Simply cutting the taxes on businesses is a good way to do that, as competitor countries have already recognised. We should do the same. And we could make company taxes very much simpler, too. At present, corporation tax is levied on a 'taxable profit' figure that bears no relation to reality, but is what you get after all the precise allowances, depreciations, reliefs and losses that Revenue & Customs allow have been deducted. It means you can end up paying the tax even when you did not actually make a profit, which is dismal. We would be much better simply taxing what companies declared and distributed on their annual accounts. One set of accounting figures would serve both purposes.

Capital taxes
Capital, like work and enterprise, is another good thing that we want more of. Saving and investing in capital goods — things like factories, machines and office equipment — enables you to produce more things in less time. It used to be that businesses had to write their customer letters out by hand, and then write another copy by hand to keep in the file. Now with computers it takes a fraction of the time, and staff are set free for more productive tasks. Again, though, we tax capital, discouraging people to save and invest and create it. Usually, we tax it in horribly complicated and time-wasting ways. Worse, the rules prompt people to invest in the lowest-tax assets, not the most productive and socially useful ones. So we are all the losers.

Capital gains tax (CGT) is one such. Many people in the UK build up small businesses over their lifetime, then sell it in order to fund their retirement. It is a perfectly natural and laudable thing to do. Until recently, they paid 10% CGT on the value that they had built up (though of course they paid corporation tax and income tax along the way, not to mention national insurance and value-added tax). Now they pay 18%. That may not sound much, but it is an 80% hike in the tax. It is hardly an incentive to encourage anyone to build a business. After all, the risk of failure is all theirs: but 18% of their success is grabbed by the state.

There is a strong case for scrapping CGT entirely. Tax economists say that some people would fiddle their earnings and call them 'capital gains' instead of salary. So, they say, the income tax rate and CGT should be the same. But they are wrong. In the first place, there would not be any investment in the UK at all if CGT rose to 40% or 50% to match income tax. Second, CGT has to be lower because we *want* people to take risks and build up businesses rather than just carry on working for someone else: that is how our economy grows. Third, there are precious few people who can switch their income between salary and capital gains anyway, so different rates are not a significant problem. As Madsen Pirie says: 'The case for a significant reduction in capital gains tax is overwhelming,' and it really would give our enterprise sector a huge boost.

Why inheritance tax is counterproductive

Inheritance tax is another tax on capital that is not only damaging, but is resented. Most parents want to leave their children a little better off than they were when their own parents died. It is entirely natural: but we go against human nature by slapping a tax on it.

The effect is that people spend a lot of time and energy trying to avoid the tax — or at least, setting things up so that their children avoid it. An army of lawyers and accountants help people set up so-called nil-rate-band trusts (don't ask) and other tax-avoidance schemes — all at a cost, of course. People take assets out of productive uses and put them into less productive investments solely to spare their children the tax. When the tax has to be paid, productive assets have to be broken up and sold to pay it.

It is crazy. Worse, it is perverse. In his 1994 Adam Smith Institute report *Will To Succeed*, tax economist Dr Barry Bracewell-Milnes calculated that for the first 105 years of their history, inheritance taxes had actually produced a *negative* return for the country. That is precisely because they encourage people to use their money less productively, and therefore thwarted the growth of business enterprises. I have no doubt that their effect is still negative today.

One fully expects politicians to pander to human envy, and to argue that rich folk should subsidise the rest of us — but not at the expense of financial common sense. The country would be better off without inheritance tax, however much envy there might be about inheritance. And there is a lot of feeling on that side too: when George Osborne announced that a Conservative government would scrap the tax for everyone except millionaires, there was a surge in the opinion polls that left even him astonished. It is human nature, after all.

Stamp duty

You pay stamp duty when you buy or sell capital assets, like shares or even your house. Gordon Brown made it characteristically complicated, with three different rates levied on house sales (which I describe as 'shocking', 'eye-watering' and 'outrageous'). Again, it makes people devise all sorts of whizzo schemes to stop themselves ending up in the higher-rate bands, helped of course by expensive lawyers and accountants. And it makes people more reluctant to sell assets and perhaps put their money into something more productive.

The burden of this tax has grown, not because we are all richer, but because inflation and the asset-price bubble put up the price of our houses. At higher prices, more tax is payable. So without being any better off, we suddenly have to pay the Treasury a lot more. That is nice for the politicians who are raking in the cash: but it is hardly an honest tax system.

Local taxes

If more powers are to be devolved from central to local government, we will have to devise some new way of raising money locally. Council tax is an unhappy compromise that rose from the ashes of the community charge — the poll tax — although that itself was built over the ruins of the almost as unpopular rates. It is a mixture of poll tax and rates, which hardly endears it to anyone. And there are limits to how much you could increase it.

If council tax were raised considerably, many people would have to sell their houses and move somewhere smaller to pay it. Many economists may think this a rational policy: it is not sound economics for pensioners to stay in their family home now that the family has gone, for example, when they could move somewhere smaller. But there is a growing number of pensioners, and to many of them, the prospect of giving up the home they have lived in for decades is both distressing and frightening.

Plainly, some new local tax is needed, either replacing council tax or in addition to it. Douglas Carswell, one of the architects of the localism idea, in his 2004 Adam Smith Institute report *Paying For Localism* advocates a local sales tax. This has many attractions, though the existence of VAT — which would be hard to remove because of EU rules — would make it complicated as yet another tax on purchases.

No system is perfect, but on deeper reflection, I think that a local income tax is probably the least worst option. If localism really is about transferring stuff from Whitehall to town hall, then an income tax is at least transparent — people would rightly expect any rise in local income tax to be offset by a fall in the national tax, and would instantly see if the total of their income taxes was rising. Second, it is easy to collect — just another line on the tax form (yes, I know I want to have as few lines on the tax form as possible, but...). The rate would be decided locally, but the tax itself would be collected by Revenue & Customs. So no new large bureaucracy would be needed: indeed, many council tax staff could be retired.

On the other hand (you can tell I trained as an economist), a tiny change in the percentage rate would make a vast difference to local revenues; so perhaps the tax is not as transparent as all that. And of course there would still have to be massive central support for some parts of the country where joblessness is high and incomes are low: so Whitehall would still be calling the shots. And with the local rate simply swept up in the national tax form, people might not even notice how much was being raised by one side or another, any more than they notice how much of their council tax is levied by the county and how much by the district. So accountability is not great under this system either.

Replacing business rates

Another part of the local finance system that we have to sort out is the rates on business properties. At present, these are largely dictated by Whitehall, because in the 1980s, Margaret Thatcher's government got alarmed by the apparent willingness of ultra-left councils (such as Derek Hatton's Liverpool) simply to milk local businesses as much as possible in order to fund extravagant spending plans. The effect, of course, was to drive firms out and create social black holes.

The Hattons have now all gone, and there is a case for denationalising business rates and letting local authorities decide their own levels. But as Richard Teather points out, there is an even stronger case for scrapping business rates altogether and instead relying on a tax on profits. At the moment, local businesses pay rates whether they are making a profit or making a loss, which causes them huge resentment, especially when they are having a hard time, laying off staff or imposing pay freezes, and then see council expenditures continuing to rise. As with income tax, such a profit tax could be collected centrally as part of a national profits tax system, with the local element decided locally and the money sent directly from the centre.

Local referendums

As I say, one problem with local taxes that are collected nationally is that they are not always completely transparent to people. So we need to build in mechanisms that increase that transparency. One method that seems to work well is the idea I mentioned earlier, of making the local authority gain the public's approval for its budget plans through a local referendum.

Many US states also have ballot initiative systems, whereby a proposal for new spending can be put to a local referendum. The rules vary from state to state, but these initiatives can be put forward by citizens themselves or by the local authority. In 2008, for example, there were 153 initiatives on the ballot in 35 states; some 61 of them came from the public and 92 came from the state governments or other public bodies. Electors, though, care about how their money is spent; and less than half of America's ballot initiatives are ever passed.

Also in the 2008 election, there were 48 initiatives and referendums to approve state budgets and tax plans. Some 15 of these failed, and the legislators had to go back to the drawing board. Now *that* is the sort of local transparency and accountability that puts our current tax system into the shade.

It seems a good motto for any government that genuinely seeks to serve the public interest, rather than its own. Read our lips: no new taxes. Not without the approval of the public in a referendum, at least.

Keeping the politicians honest

I am conscious that once we have scaled down or swept away all these pernicious, distorting, incentive-crushing taxes, the machinery of government will be a little short of financial fuel. But then my friend Lado Gurgenidze is right: you do need to keep government short of money to keep its attention focused on what it really does need to do.

Think about it. If you or I could simply go up to our neighbours and demand money from them, and put them in jail if they did not give it to us, it is likely that our spending would get slightly reckless too. We would not worry too much about the cost of things, being surrounded by walking piggy banks that we could dip in to any time we wanted. They might squeal a bit every five years at elections, but that is not too difficult to bear.

That is why we need some long-stop control on the nation's tax policy, just as we have an independent panel deciding monetary policy and interest rates. The size of the tax burden may be a political issue, but it is one that is too important to be decided by populist politicians alone. We either have a new quango to make sure that governments manage their budgets responsibly, or we have a set of agreed constitutional limits on spending and borrowing. I know which I would prefer.

CONCLUSION

'The rot starts from the top,' wrote commentator Will Hutton in his 1995 book *The State We're In*. How right he was. And how naïve to think that a few years of New Labour cosmetic surgery could repair it. For — as is now all too obvious — it was the political class itself that was infecting us and weakening us. With landslide majorities, they really did believe that they were in perfect tune with the views of 'The People' (though in fact, fewer and fewer of 'the people' thought them even worth bothering to turn out and vote for at elections: more people voted in TV's *X Factor* competition than voted for the Blair-Brown governments). Yet, fortified by this spirit of self-belief, they became supremely confident of their ability to heal the nation's ills, and in their unique authority to do so.

Accordingly, they absorbed more and more power to the centre. New laws, rules, regulations and targets were issued, at increasing pace. The politicians assured us that they were getting on with the job of restoring us to health.

In fact, all this centralisation of power has starved civil society of its life-blood. Functions that were once done willingly and freely by individuals have been taken over by the state or hidebound by bureaucratic rules. The whole creative energy of civil society's informal and inclusive local networks, associations, movements, voluntary groups — even families — has been slowly drained away to Westminster and Whitehall. Under the weight of direction from this distant, uninvolved bureaucracy, villages can no longer organise charity duck races without undertaking full risk assessments, parents are banned from school sports events unless they have Criminal Records Bureau checks to prove they are not paedophiles or kidnappers, and church wardens have to undergo training on how to use a stepladder before they can change a light bulb in the nave.

Our many and obvious ills will never be healed while our political leaders deny individuals and families the space to breathe. It can happen only if we slacken the tourniquet of centralised power and throw off the choking cotton wool of the nanny state. But the rot has spread widely, into almost every area of public life. We *can* stop the rot, and although we all know that it has gone so far that any effective surgery will be painful, we also know that it is essential, and we are up for it. Indeed, the public are more willing to endure the pain than our politicians seem willing to inflict it. But that is politics: the hard things that need to be done are put off because politicians are not brave enough to put the straight facts to the electorate, denying that there is anything wrong at all, or telling us that a temporary patch-up will work just fine. Unfortunately, we need more than a temporary patch-up. We need to get to the heart of the government sector, and ask afresh what exactly it should do, and where it should simply butt out.

Getting ourselves out of debt
Our economic condition is grave. Our national debt is as high

as it was after Waterloo or VE Day, when at least it bought us victory over tyrants. Today's massive debt has bought us no more than bloated public services and a few dud banks. Even on the government's own figures, which are consistently and notoriously optimistic, its debts will carry on rising until 2015. Many economists see them rising even longer.

It is a fundamental rule of life, which every family and business is well aware of, that when you are crippled by debt you need to spend less or earn more. Things are no different for government. They either have to pull in more money from taxation, or rein in what they spend. Neither is an attractive option to politicians who have the press and the opinion polls hounding them, of course. But the public knows the score well enough. It is long past time for the political class to be frank with us.

The frank story, of course, is that our government has spent and borrowed far too much. It has expanded the public sector by half, using money that it has either borrowed or sneaked from our pockets in stealth taxes. If it had all gone into better public services, we might have something good to show for it. But the tsunami of cash has hit public services so hard and so fast that they have been completely unable to spend it efficiently. They have paid themselves higher wages, of course, but their productivity has actually declined.

The last thing we want now is a hair of the dog — carrying on as before, trying to spend or even borrow our way out of debt. We need to reduce public spending hard and fast. That does not mean across-the-board cuts or firing front-line teachers or doctors. But it does mean looking systematically at government does, identifying what it does not need to do, working out what others can do better, and then thinking afresh on what it should look like. This is not a job for penny-pinching Treasury ministers, whom nobody will trust. It is a job for a dedicated public service reform team.

Being honest about the financial crisis

It would be easier to solve the financial crisis too, if our politicians were honest about its causes. They have rushed to blame the 'greed' of bankers for our ills, when the blame rests squarely on themselves. For two decades, authorities in both the UK and the United States were flooding the world with cheap money. Whatever crisis came along — the 1987 stock market crash, the 1989 Russian debt default, 9/11 — they staved off the downturn by slashing interest rates. So we all took out cheap loans and bought houses, which then rose in price, prompting us to do even more of the same. (In that sense, we borrowers were just as 'greedy' as the banks who lent to us, but of course no politicians want to criticise their electors.)

As the boom continued, the politicians thought they really had abolished boom and bust. But eventually the bust came, as it had to. You cannot build real prosperity on fake money.

The crisis has been a convenient excuse for everyone who wants to beat up capitalism — and EU leaders who envy London's position as Europe's only truly international financial market — to propose supra-national regulation of the banks. That is the last thing we need. Bureaucratic regulation has already made our banks too big: small ones just cannot afford its cost. Instead, we need banks that are smaller, so they do not bring down the whole system when they get into difficulties. The government must break up the banks and lighten the regulation on them to compensate.

Then get out of the business entirely. Politicians are rubbish at running the nation's commerce.

Reforming a dysfunctional Parliament

Actually it is hard to know what politicians *are* good at, other than fiddling their expenses or giving themselves perks. No wonder they have lost our trust.

Yet the problem is deeper still. Parliament is no longer fit for purpose. Around a fifth of our MPs are ministers and officials on the government payroll: they are never going to vote against the government line. Not just their salaries, but their chauffeur cars, swank official apartments and gold-plated pensions depend on it. MPs are supposed to represent *us* — but too many of them represent their own careers, their personal finance, or whatever the party apparatchiks and spin doctors in Downing Street deem fitting.

We could survive with far fewer MPs — other countries do — and far, far fewer ministers. Before long, we should boot ministers out of Parliament entirely, and have a US-style separation of powers. We should tell the party machines to get lost and select parliamentary candidates by open hustings. We must focus MPs' time on the really important issues — like scrutinising EU regulations — rather than on the details of road closures or the size of eggs. And we need to devolve much more power down from Westminster to the local authorities and better, down to the people themselves, from whom it ultimately springs.

Curbing the bureaucracy

Like MPs, Whitehall bureaucrats are not short of a bob or two, particularly with those generous inflation-proofed pensions that let them retire on two-thirds of their salary. You or I would have to save over £1 million to get the same pension as a senior (not even top-ranking) civil servant. In total, taxpayers will shell out £1 trillion (yes, that is £1,000,000,000,000) to pay the pensions of these faithful retainers — mandarins, teachers, doctors, police officers, firefighters, council bureaucrats and all the rest. Given the financial pickle we are in, any government that cannot get to grips with this scam should be sacked. The whole fraud needs to end right now, with public servants being moved on to pension arrangements more in line with what the rest of us have — which is not a lot.

Another outrage is the mushrooming growth of the quangos — all those boards, committees, regulators and advisory panels. Their numbers and cost have simply exploded. In many sectors, like health and education, there are so many of them that they get under each other's feet. They dump vast paperwork costs on struggling private businesses. Some even have the power to fine companies and charge them fees for their 'service'. And of course they are largely unaccountable.

The quangos must be curbed. We could send them all home and hardly anyone would even notice, but it would at least give us some time to decide which were worth keeping. If any survive, they should have a maximum five-year life, so that it takes a conscious decision by Parliament to keep them going. And they should report to MPs, the people's representatives, not to all-powerful ministers.

The most effective discipline on the public sector, though, would be to make it post online everything it buys. If people could see how much of our money the state is spending, and on what, they would be less willing to put up with bureaucracy and waste. Private firms could tell us when they could do the same job for half the price. Back-handers and nepotism would be exposed. And it would focus civil-service minds on getting value for money.

Creating new quality schools

The fact that 98% of school kids pass their GCSEs looks impressive, until you discover that in maths, 9 out of 100 gets you a pass. That is why nobody trusts our examination system any more than they trust the politicians who run it — neither parents, nor universities, nor employers. It may also be why one in ten of us have significant literacy problems — not a promising foundation on which to build the UK's economic and social recovery.

If parents had a real choice about which school their kids went to, they would not put up with the fake education served up by the state education monopoly. They would want genuine education, and the best education. But today, only the rich can afford to go private and get that.

We need to give all parents that purchasing power. Sweden has a good way of doing it — one that is now universally popular, even among the left who originally opposed it. In Sweden, education is still free, and the government still pays: but the money follows *your* choices, not the bureaucrats' choices. Put your child into a school that you think better, and that school gets your child's bit of the education budget. Indeed, parents and teachers, fed up with bad schools, have even built their own schools to take advantage of the new policy.

No top-up fees, no selection, everyone treated equally, but people genuinely able to choose *whatever* school they think best for their child. The idea revolutionised education in Sweden in less than a decade. It will do the same here too.

Opening up healthcare choices

Politicians of all parties tell us that we love the National Health Service (NHS) and that they will protect it for us. Well, we might love our *healthcare* — and as we get older, we know we need to spend more on it. But we are much more sceptical about spending more and more money on the *NHS*, venerable institution though it is. Millions of us buy private insurance, and even more go private for their operations, often dipping into their 'rainy day' money to pay for it. Hardly an overwhelming vote of confidence in state healthcare. We are paying half as much again to the NHS as we were just a decade ago; but the tales of hospital-acquired superbugs and patients waiting in ambulances so as not to offend some government target are eroding our trust.

We need to break up the NHS's double monopoly of finance and provision. The easiest way is to put GPs in charge of our bit of the healthcare budget, and allow them to buy in our care from whatever provider suited us, public of private.

Ultimately, though, we need to move to a more European-style healthcare system, where we give people a choice of insurance funds, instead of forcing everyone into one single funding system. The service can stay free, and we can give patients the choice of where they are treated — in the public, private, or voluntary sectors. Then, at last, our healthcare system would focus on the needs of patients, rather than on the need to comply with some political target.

Work is the best anti-poverty programme

Our welfare system is not just creaky. It is completely dys-functional. It subsidises the very things we want to discourage and taxes the very things we want to promote. It traps people on benefits and in unemployment by confiscating up to 90% of the money they earn by getting a job. Most criminal of all, it leaves couples better off splitting up than staying together.

The complex array of different benefits, all with different rules, is a bureaucratic nightmare that produces utter chaos. It should be stripped down to just two benefits at the most; and those should be integrated with taxes so that people are always better off getting a job, and then getting a better job.

As many countries have discovered, benefits need to come with responsibilities. They need to depend on claimants doing at least something to get themselves off benefits and into *work* — the best anti-poverty device yet devised by humankind.

Redefining the role of state and citizen

The politicians' centralisation of state power has killed our trust in the justice system too. Today, people are more likely to see the police as agents of the state rather than servants of the public. That is not surprising when they can no longer stop you and ask a friendly question about what you are up to, but have to record the whole process, plus your personal details, on forms that get sent up to some police computer where the incident will be filed forever. We must make the police far more accountable to the local communities that they serve, and far less driven by the targets and paperwork dreamed up by Home Office ministers and officials.

Most crime, that same Home Office thinks, is drug related. But recreational drug users create almost no problem at all: the crime comes from people with real drug problems and chaotic lives. Years of being 'tough on drugs' has not worked: the problem has grown. The right policy is to treat those with heroin and other addictions as *patients* who should be helped by our healthcare system, rather than as *criminals* who should be jailed by our justice system. Get that problem out of the way and you can safely decriminalise recreational drugs and, by opening up the whole underworld, cut crime too.

Staggering numbers of our legal rights — trial by jury, habeas corpus, the presumption of innocence — have been suspended by new laws in just the last decade or so. Often, the justification is convincing — the authorities need strong powers to save us from terrorism, say — but the effect is the same: to leave us without protection against those in power. And power, of course, corrupts. This is not a situation that can be sorted out by just passing a law to reverse a few of the worst abuses. It needs a full-scale review of our rights and liberties, and a national debate on the relationship between the state and the citizen that puts the citizen firmly back in charge.

Reining in the bully state

The antics of the nanny state, as it bans balloons outside shops for health and safety reasons, or declares garden gnomes a fire hazard, gives the nation much innocent amusement; but the state has moved well beyond nannying. It is now into bullying. Many politicians would like to record all of our details on a national database. The police would love to have DNA swabs from every one of us (and like to add to their sample collection by arresting innocent people for no good reason at all). Local authorities use anti-terrorist legislation to spy on our wheelie-bin habits. Even supposedly 'liberal' politicians want to 'nudge' us into doing what they think best, rather than believing that we can make our own minds up, thank you very much.

Again, just reversing a few measures like ID cards, or telling the police to junk the DNA samples of innocent people after six months, or suggesting to councils that they should reserve anti-terrorist legislation for its proper purpose, will not stop the rot. Before long they will find some other way of doing exactly the same again. Rather, we need a full-scale review and national debate on our rights and liberties, leading to a thoroughgoing set of rules of justice that will safeguard us from our rulers for many years to come.

Confining regulation to a purpose

Our social and economic lives are hidebound by rules and regulations of one sort or another. Nearly three-quarters of them come from Brussels, but Whitehall also likes to think up new rules for us, as do the regulators themselves (I suppose they need to justify their existence). But regulation adds huge cost to business, which makes it harder for new firms to start up, reduces competition, and leaves the public with a worse deal. And all too often, it is the poor who pay most of the cost.

This is another area where Parliament fails us. With about 3,500 new regulations going through every year, MPs cannot see the wood for the trees. They need to separate out the trivial ones from the important ones, and debate the latter. They must challenge EU regulations early, before they become a done deal. Perhaps a reformed House of Lords could take on the job if the Commons was too busy discussing road closures and suchlike.

We need to tackle all the sources of regulation on three fronts. First, is new regulation really necessary? Second, is existing regulation working or — as is usually the case — is it counterproductive? How much existing regulation can we simply consolidate or scrap? Third, how rigidly should different regulations be enforced? One of those things that alienates the public from officialdom is its frequent tendency to use its state sledgehammers on our nuts.

Taxes

And they say we should be happy to pay taxes for all this. Frankly, I could be happy for half the money. We now work solidly for more than four months each year, solely to pay the demands of the tax collectors. Add in the burden of the government's borrowing, and it is over five months of each year. That is higher than it has been in decades. High taxes are a sure way of scaring jobs abroad, where entrepreneurs can get a better return on their talents and investments.

The complexity of our tax system is no help either. Income tax and national insurance are pretty similar taxes, but their rules are widely different, making them unfathomable to small businesses and the general public. We should follow the example of a growing number of countries and strip out all complexity, all the complicated reliefs and thresholds, and instead have a flat rate tax of, say, just 20%. While we are at it, we should take everyone on the minimum wage out of tax entirely: it is daft that people on just a fraction of the average income should be paying tax, and it puts people off leaving benefits and joining the workforce.

Paradoxically, high earners would actually pay more tax if the top rates of tax were cut or eliminated. Wherever that has happened before, they always have. Instead of employing expensive accountants or shipping their money or themselves off to some tax haven, they are quite willing to pay tax at reasonable rates. If we want to generate the enterprise to lift us out of our present financial hole, it is exactly the world's mobile high-fliers that we want to come here, stay here and invest here.

Time to think radically
This is, of course, a radical manifesto; but the times call for radical measures. Deep rot has set in to our economic position, and we need to balance the books again, and do it now. Decay has set into our social life, and we need to sort out our public services and our welfare system afresh, making them focused and cost-effective. Our constitution has putrefied, with the state usurping the rights and freedoms of citizens. Our state institutions have been corrupted by a politicised centre that drains power and energy from civil society. And our trust in authority has perished as we see politicians, public officials and even the police serving their own interests rather than ours. Stopping the rot and renewing Britain will not be pleasant nor easy; but we need to do it, urgently and effectively.

Also available:

Londonistan, Melanie Phillips

Time to Emigrate?, George Walden

Whose Side Are They On? How Big Brother Government Is Ruining Britain, Alan Pearce

It's Health and Safety Gone Mad! 1001 Crazy Safety Crimes, Alan Pearce

China: A Wolf in the World?, George Walden

House of Bush House of Saud: The Secret Relationship between the World's Two Most Powerful Dynasties, Craig Unger

Blowing up Russia, Alexander Litvinenko and Yuri Felshtinsky